THE
SHASTA INDIANS
OF CALIFORNIA
AND THEIR NEIGHBORS

by
ELIZABETH RENFRO

Illustration by R.J.SHEPPARD

Library of Congress Cataloging-in-Publication Data:

Renfro, Elisabeth.
  The Shasta Indians of California and ther neighbors / by
Elizabeth Refro.
      p.   cm.
  Includes bibliographical references.
  1. Shastan Indians.   I. Title.
  E99.S332R46   1992
  979.4'004975--dc20   92-20065
                                                                  CIP
ISBN-13: 978-087961-221-4
ISBN-10: 0-87961-221-5

Cover painting and illustrations by R. J. Sheppard

Seventh printing 2009

Naturegraph Publishers has been publishing books on
natural history, Native Americans, and outdoor subjects since
1946. Please write for our free catalog.

Books for a better world

Naturegraph Publishers, Inc.
PO Box 1047 ● 3543 Indian Creek Rd.
Happy Camp, CA 96039
(530) 493-5353
www.naturegraph.com

Acknowledgements

I thought first to dedicate this book to Miss Clara Wicks (1879–1978), a Scott Valley Shasta, and her descendants. But that is too presumptuous. Miss Wicks, through her gifts of lectures and stories to groups all over Siskiyou County, and through her work with Shasta Nation organizers and with researchers from the University of California and other institutions, gave people more of the Shasta culture and its spirit than a book this size can do justice to.

So instead, I wish to simply give my thanks indirectly to Miss Clara Wicks and directly to her nephew Tom Webster and his wife Bess, who shared with me Aunt Clara's tapes, photographs, and artifacts, as well as their own memories of that remarkable woman. The Websters gave much of their own time and efforts during my research, including helping me make contact with many other people who generously shared their memories, newspaper clippings, photographs, artifacts, and their own research. I extend heartfelt thanks to all of these people, and most especially to Tom and Bess Webster, without whose encouragement this book would not have been completed.

Elizabeth Renfro

Table of Contents

Introduction

A Creation Story[*]

I

One day Waka, the Great Spirit, Old Man Above, tired of his dwelling place in the clouds. He looked down, through a hole he had made in the clouds, at the barren earth below. "I will make a new land below," he said.

But it was too far for him to step down from the cloud to the land, so Waka pushed rocks, ice, and snow through the hole, and more, and more, until the mound grew high enough for him to step to it, to walk down its sides to the earth below. Waka saw this mountain was shining and white, and so he named it *Wyeka*, "pure white," and he chose it for his home.

Then Waka turned to the barren land around Wyeka. He called for trees to grow, and tall and straight grew pines, cottonwoods, cedar, and oaks. That they might drink he called the sun to melt snow from Wyeka, and the sun did as Waka asked, and streams flowed clear and swift.

Waka saw that this new world needed creatures. He took leaves from the trees and blew them from his open hand: crows, bluejays, eagles, herons, and doves flew into the skies. He broke bits of wood

---

[*] This Creation story is also ascribed to the Modoc, Karuk, Wintu.

from a stick, tossed the pieces in the streams, and trout and salmon swam the waters.

Then Waka looked to the land and said, "A land needs creatures to live on it." So he took up his staff. From the narrow end of it he carved off some wood, and beavers, moles, squirrels, and raccoons ran through the brush. From the strong midsection of his staff Waka carved, and foxes, coyotes, deer, and bobcats ran through the forest.

Then Waka carved from the head of his staff, and Lord Grizzly, strong and wise, stood at the foot of the mountain. Old Man Above charged him to rule the lands about Wyeka. And Waka went to live in his icy tent, to warm his hands at its fire, which still sends smoke curling up into the sky.

II.

One day Great Wind blew too fiercely about Wyeka's sides. Waka, the Great Spirit, sent his youngest daughter to the smokehole to ask Great Wind to pass gently over their home. He warned her to call just from the smokehole's rim, not to push her head above Wyeka's folds.

The youngest daughter went and called to Great Wind at the smokehole as she was bid. But she raised her head above the smokehole's edge. Great Wind grabbed her by her long, flying hair and carried her out of Wyeka's shelter and down to the forest lands below.

There Waka's daughter was found by Lord Grizzly as he was hunting. He took up the shivering child and carried her home to the warmth of his fire. There Mother Grizzly stroked the smooth red child and said, "I will raise her with our children."

Waka's daughter lived and grew up with the grizzlies, and when she came of age, she mated with Lord Grizzly's oldest son. Their children were strong and tall like the grizzlies, smooth-skinned and fair like the daughter of Wyeka. The grizzlies built for them a lodge, *Wahkalu* [Shastina] at Wyeka's foot, that Waka's daughter might have a fit home.

One day a cloud hovered over Wyeka's smokehole and called down to the Great Spirit that his daughter lived, that the grizzlies had kept and reared her. Waka ran down Wyeka's side (the marks of his footsteps linger still) to seek her.

When he saw his daughter surrounded by the new race she and the grizzlies had created, his anger was great. He smote Mother Grizzly dead with a frown. The grizzlies he sentenced: "Henceforth you must go on four legs, never to speak again, never to rise up but in fear." And the children, the new race, he drove from their lodge into the forest and sealed forever Wahkalu's doors.

His daughter he took home to Wyeka.

The Shastan Tribes [*]

Wyeka, or Mount Shasta, dominates the landscape in northern California. Located forty miles from the Oregon border, the 14,000 foot mountain has been revered by Indians for thousands of years, and even today inspires lore and worship. Today's name for the mountain, Shasta, was the name of an Indian chief of the area, and it is the name of one of those tribes that made the mountain's

---

[*] In my use of the three terms *Shastan, Shasta,* and *Shastas,* I have tried to achieve a compromise between the versions used by ethnographers (though their use, too, varies) and the terms as I heard them used by contemporary Shasta. Ethnographers have used *Shastan* primarily in adjectival form, modifying such nouns as "people" and "tribes." The term refers to the common language (albeit comprised of several dialects) shared by these distinct bands or tribes (Okwanuchu, New River Shasta, Konomihu, Rogue River Shasta, and Shasta), and I have used it only in that descriptive sense. Contemporary Shasta use the term *Shasta* for their people, and consider all the bands, or tribes, part of the Shasta Nation. *Shastas* is used (by Shastas with whom I've spoken and in this book) to show individual distinction, to show the concept of individualization of Shastas within the inclusive Shasta Nation.

surrounding lands their home. Today the same name, Shasta, is also used to describe the four tribes that originally inhabited this area.

Up until one hundred and fifty years ago, the forests and river valleys surrounding Mt. Shasta were home to thousands of Shastan-speaking Indians. They were a unique and sizable group of American Indians whose culture reflected a blend of Central Californian, Great Basin, and Pacific Coastal characteristics, as well as its own individuality. However, even given the numbers of Shastan people before white contact and the fullness of their culture, most Americans have read and heard comparatively little about the aboriginal culture of these people who lived in the shadow of Wyeka, or about the Shasta today who still live on their ancestral lands.

Anthropologists and ethnographers have estimated the population of Shastan-speaking people in the 1840s at about 2,000–3,000, a number many of today's Shastas consider far too low. There is evidence for a higher pre-contact population. Consider that lists of Shastan villages made after the turn of this century, based almost solely on a few informants' memories, cite over one hundred and fifty separate villages. These informants, even when describing villages no longer existent during their own lifetimes, would have been describing the tribe after the first white contact (i. e., trappers and explorers) brought diseases such as measles and smallpox, which wiped out whole villages. Even bearing in mind that most communities were small (twenty-five to forty inhabitants), the figure of 10,000 used by some contemporary Shastas for pre-contact population does not seem unreasonable.

The Shasta have been described in contemporary times as represented by a handful of mixed heritage survivors, with their language and culture "on the verge of extinction" (Silver 1978, 212), and three of the four Shastan-speaking tribes were listed as completely wiped out around the beginning of the twentieth century when A. L. Kroeber wrote his exhaustive *Handbook of the Indians of California*. But this is misleading.

Much of their culture does survive, particularly if "culture" is viewed not as a static aboriginal picture but as a living, growing, and adapting set of values and beliefs. Today's Shasta Nation includes a formal roll of more than 1200 members, comprising descendants of Shasta Valley, Scott Valley, and Klamath River bands of Shasta, as well as Okwanuchu, Konomihu, and New River Shasta descendants. The tribe has a practicing medicine woman, and as a nation it is actively involved in pursuing federal recognition, as well as working with the United States Forest Service to revise and correct the record on their people. Shastas today pursue careers, in their traditional lands and elsewhere, in farming, ranching, teaching, business, and medicine, among other things.

About This Book

Because the culture of the Shastan tribes was so quickly and deeply disrupted in the second half of the nineteenth century, accounts of the pre-contact Shastan tribes are few and often sketchy and contradictory. The information gathered by anthropologists and ethnographers is always limited by the number of informants, by those informants' justifiable reluctance to reveal certain sacred or private aspects of the culture, and, of course, by each researcher's own often unconscious beliefs and biases.

What I have tried to present in this book is an honest and fairly objective overview of a people and culture, both its aboriginal and its contemporary elements, based on materials and evidence available to me. In the narrative sections in chapter 2, which are entirely imaginary, I have incorporated information based upon Shasta informants' accounts, particularly those of Miss Clara Wicks, in an attempt to recreate the tenor of aboriginal Shasta life.

In the course of researching this book, I sought out both written material and Shastan people themselves. The written material ranged from early ethnographic reports to newspaper accounts of white/Indian clashes, to reports of the United States Department of Forestry, to unpublished field notes, tapes, and library collections (see the bibliography at the end of this book). So much material is available that this book must be recognized as only a brief overview of the Shasta, of their history with the whites, and of their efforts over the years to maintain their culture. Much remains to be researched and presented about these people.

I know full well, and hope readers will also be aware, that there can be no "final word" on a people and a culture, whether on their present condition or on their past, and that the work of an outsider to that culture, while it may bring a wider or more objective view, must always be viewed with an awareness of its inherent limitations.

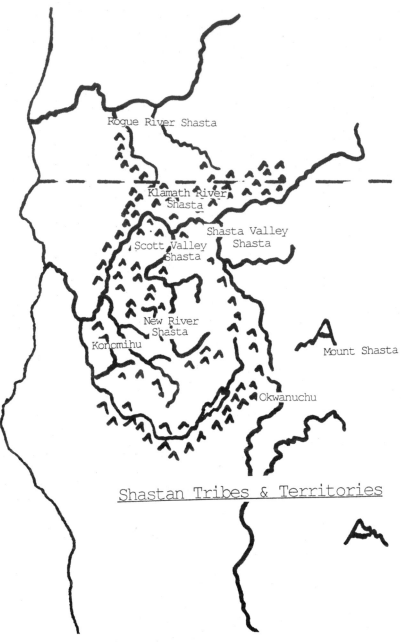

Figure 1. Shastan tribes and territories.

Chapter 1

The Shastan Tribes:

Their Place Among California Indians

California Indian groups, the Shasta included, have always been difficult to classify because of the number of tribes and the diversity of dialects and cultures. The word "tribe" is difficult to use in reference to California Indian groups, since many of the groups speaking the same language or dialect acted quite independently of one another. Even the more unified groups of California Indians did not have the sense of tribal unity that, for example, the Sioux Nation showed. An abundant food supply coupled with minimal warring between the California tribes did not demand the same high degree of organization.

Because of this lack of formal organization, anthropologists have generally classified the various California tribes according to similar linguistic characteristics. The language of the Shastan tribes places them as a part of the great Hokan language group, which connects them in origin with California's Karuk, Yana, and Pomo in the north, the Achomawi and Washo in the east, and the Esselen, Salinan, Chumash, and Yuman to the south.

The Hokan-speaking peoples are thought to have been the original settlers of California, coming across the Bering Straits from Asia about 10,000 years ago. Although the Shasta are the northernmost of the Hokan groups in California, some anthropological studies indicate that their presence is the result of later migration north by Hokan-speaking peoples who had settled earlier in central and southern California. Stephen Powers (1877) cites a "Shastika" tradition that their people migrated to their territory from the north/northwest; but, according to the majority of accounts, the Shasta themselves have no tribal, historical, or mythological account of migration, and consider their aboriginal lands and their people to have been created expressly for one another.

In addition to their connections to the Hokan stock, the Shastan tribes show cultural affinities with neighboring tribes, particularly with the Karuk, Yurok, and Hupa toward the coast; the Wintu, an interior California tribe to the south; the Klamath to the north; and the Modoc of the Great Basin culture group to the east.

As A. L. Kroeber ([1925] 1976, 281-82) wrote of the Shasta in his *Handbook of the Indians of California*: "In this vicinity...four great stocks meet and touch: the Athabascans, as represented by the Hupa...; the Algonquins, in the shape of their most westerly branch, the Yurok and Wiyot; the Penutians, of whom the Wintun are the most northerly...in California; and the Hokan family, of whose many far-stretched divisions...the Shastans are the extreme northern representative....It is clear that this extraordinary agglomeration not only has meaning but it bears a significance which may someday carry us back into remote periods."

Based on both linguistic and cultural elements, the Shastan group itself is generally considered to include three small tribes and one large tribe. Some anthropologists disagree on this, but today's Shasta Nation includes these four tribes in their self-definition.

The large tribe is the Shastas, which is further divided into four or five bands based upon dialectal and generally minor cultural differences, as well as geographical locations. The Ahotireitsu lived in Shasta Valley, the Iruaitsu in Scott Valley, the Katiru or Wiruwhitsu along the Klamath River, and the Ikiruka'tsu along the Rogue River. The names of these bands vary according to the dialect of the informant, as each band had its own name for the other bands, as well as for itself.

The three smaller tribes are the Okwanuchu, the New River Shasta, and the Konomihu. Some ethnographers also include with the Shastan tribes the Kammatwa (or Gamutwa) and the Watido (or Watiru) who primarily lived between the Scott River and Seiad Valley, but who spoke a dialect distinct from the other Shasta. Other accounts suggest that the Kammatwa and Watido might have been parts of the smaller Shastan-speaking tribes.

To the south and southeast there were three other closely related tribes also belonging to the Hokan group: the Chimariko, the Atsugewi, and the Achomawi. These three tribes were originally classed as branches of the Shastan group, but as a result of later linguistic and cultural studies they are generally not included in it, and they are not considered Shastan by today's Shasta Nation.

The source of the name "Shasta" is unclear. Some accounts say that it is derived from the name of a prominent chief who lived near the gold mining center of Yreka in the 1850s, whose name is variously transcribed as "Sasti," "Sustika," and "Shastika." However, an account from Peter Skene Odgen's expedition in 1827 (before Chief Sasti's time) refers to a tribe of Indians to the south whom the Oregon Klamath Indians called "Sastise" or "Shasty."

As is true of most Native American groups, who have no generic word for "Indian," the Shasta placed greater importance on the identification of individual bands. Some sources list "Kahosadi" as a tribal name, though other sources explain that this name identifies only the Oregon Shasta band. The same is true of the name "Gikats," or "Kakatsik," which is given by some sources as the full tribal name.

In numbers, both before and after the appearance of the *pastin*, or whites, the members of the Shasta bands were dominant among the Shastan peoples. Using the prevailing published estimates of a total Shastan population of 3,000 in pre-white times, 2,000 were

The Shasta River, about two miles south of Montague.

The Scott River, about half a mile north of Callahan.

The Klamath River at Horse Creek.

Shastas. By 1906, an estimated 121 Shastas were still living in Siskiyou County; fewer than forty were recorded in 1962. The other three tribes had estimated populations of roughly 300 each in 1850, with some records showing none in existence by the 1920s. Again, however, these figures are open to dispute, and by many accounts should be much higher.

The lands once occupied by thousands of Shastan peoples are still lovely today, even after years of mining and ranching use. But two hundred and more years ago, those lands were extraordinary for their riches and variety: forested mountains with bear, deer, and elk; river valleys with flourishing edible plant life, mussels, salmon, trout, and other fishes, as well as small valley animals; and lava beds providing obsidian for knives and arrowheads.

The Shastan tribes roamed a territory that reached north to the Rogue River in southern Oregon; west to the Klamath Mountain range and the Salmon River and New River forks; east in Oregon to Mt. Pitt and in California to Mt. Shasta; and south to just below Mt. Shasta. The wealth of this land freed the Shastan peoples from the near-constant hunger experienced by the Great Basin tribes and by some of the other California tribes, and it allowed them to trade foodstuffs and craft items to other tribes in exchange for luxury items like shells and fancy basketry. The variety of natural bounty in all seasons kept the Shasta in close communion with the land's cycles.

Because the Shastan peoples moved with the bounty of the seasons, tribal "boundaries" were constantly shifting to some extent. The basic territory for the largest Shastan tribe, the Shastas, was roughly north and west of Mt. Shasta, with settlements primarily in the valleys along the lower Rogue and Klamath rivers, and along the Scott and Shasta rivers. The Shastas were bordered to the north by Oregon's Klamath and Takelma tribes, with whom they traded dried acorn paste for dentalia shells, the primary form of money used by all the Indian tribes along the Pacific Coast. To the west and southwest the Shasta were bounded by the Karuk and Hupa, to whom they provided pine nuts, juniper beads, deer skins, and obsidian blades in exchange for acorns, baskets, dentalia and other shells, and, occasionally, canoes. To the east of the Shastas were the warlike Modoc, with whom little trade was carried on. The Shastas feared the Modoc, who often raided Shasta villages for slaves, and the Shastas sometimes carried out retaliatory raids.

To the south of the Shastas lived the three other Shastan tribes, the New River Shasta, the Konomihu, and the Okwanuchu. All of these tribes were poorer than the Shastas, so little trade was carried on with them, though the Shastas did pass traded goods on to these tribes. Similarly, little trade was carried on with the Chimariko, the Achomawi, and the Atsugewi to the southeast.

The Okwanuchu, who lived just south of Mt. Shasta, established their villages primarily along the Salt and Squaw Valley creeks, near the headwaters of the Sacramento River. They were bounded by the Shastas to the north, the Modoc to the northeast, the Achomawi to the east, and the Wintu to the south and west.

The territories of the New River Shasta and the Konomihu are not known with any certainty, and ethnographers give differing and even contradictory accounts of the tribes' boundaries. The villages and hunting and gathering grounds of the New River Shasta were roughly in the area between the Salmon Mountains and the Salmon River's north fork. South and slightly west, according to most accounts, were the Konomihu, whose home lands were near the north forks of the New River and the Salmon River's north and south forks. These two small Shastan tribes had the Karuk and the Hupa to the east, the Chimariko and Wintu to the south and southeast, and the Shastas to the north and northeast.

It must be noted that all of these "boundaries" are estimates. Because of the genocide practiced against the Shastan tribes by miners, settlers, and even the United States government, coupled with the minimal archaeological work done (most of it not until the 1960s), little concrete data is available. Some contemporary Shasta cite traditional accounts of Shasta settlements near Clear Creek, below Happy Camp to the west (Winthrop 1986, 76), and as far east as the Klamath River Canyon below Big Bend.

Even as widely spread as they were, the Shastan tribes, especially the large Shasta tribe, showed a greater degree of tribal unity than did many of the widely diversified tribes in California, particularly more than their western neighbors, the Karuk, Yurok, and Hupa, where even a village did not necessarily act as a unified group.

All four of the Shastan tribes had chiefs, and the Shastas themselves had a chief for each of their four major subtribes. Some accounts state that the Rogue River Shasta chief was the head or the most highly respected of the four.

Still, the basic spirit of independence and the closely bound lifestyle of the individual settlements demanded family "subchiefs" who handled day-to-day affairs. Thus, individual villages operated with autonomy, which is characteristic of most California Indian groups.

The existent tribal organization among the Shastan tribes, political and social, was both practical and humanitarian. In addition to its allowance for individual autonomy, it showed an interesting blend of what we today would call materialistic, capitalistic, and socialistic elements. The political and social organization reflected the value the Shastan peoples placed upon peace, individual worth, human life, and upon a sense of community and natural responsibility for others.

Chiefs were chosen by a combination of factors, including hereditary lines to previous chiefs, wealth, and the group's common consent as a result of a leader's demonstrated mediation abilities. Wealth and eloquence were of major importance because a chief's duties were twofold. First, in a daily prayer-chant he reminded the people of their duties to go in peace, to have kind and generous hearts, and to be industrious. He also had the task of resolving, by convincing all involved parties to accept his arrangements, all disputes ranging from trespassing to murder. Second, the chief had the final responsibility for all levied fines, so that if a member of his village were unable to pay a charged fine, the chief would pay it for him in order to maintain peace and harmony.

All intratribe disputes were handled by this system of payment to the victim or the victim's family, and if private revenge were taken, the revenge-taker was held culpable for wrongdoing. Amounts levied varied, of course, with the offense, but all payments were tied to a scale of each individual's monetary worth, which was determined by the bride-price paid for his or her mother. At first glance, the decreeing of an individual's value in monetary terms may sound cold-hearted and calculated. The system did, however, accord with the Shasta's generally noncombative nature, and it protected community harmony and lives. In a situation where an individual could not simply move away if angry, and where all members of the community were interdependent upon one another for food and safety, an effective, clearcut system of recompense that could avoid bloodshed and feuds was vital.

Today's Shasta Nation (as of 1986) lists over 1200 persons on its rolls, over 300 of whom live on their ancestral lands. These Shasta are descendants of the Okwanuchu, Konomihu, New River, and California-Oregon Shasta. Members of the Oregon branch, the Rogue River Shasta who remained north, are listed on the rolls of the Confederated Tribes of Grande Ronde [Reservation] and the Confederated Tribes of Siletz [Reservation] because of the separate treaty they signed after the Rogue River Wars.

Since the late 1970s, the Shasta have been increasingly active in organizing their tribe for political activity. The formation in 1982 of the Shasta Tribe, Incorporated, a nonprofit, public benefit corporation, was one of their major steps toward a contemporary organizational format that would give the Nation the legal status it needs in its continuing work to gain federal recognition, fight desecration of their traditional lands, and maintain the traditional lifeways.

Chapter 2

Before the Pastin:
Pre-Contact Lifeways

Before white explorers, miners, and settlers (*pastin*) disrupted their traditional lifeways, the Shastan peoples lived in a world centered around three interlocking and interdependent elements: nature (particularly their traditional lands), family, and beliefs. This holistic approach to life meant that the extended family unit was the center of Shasta life, that all activities were a part of a natural ritual, and that all ritual was a natural part of life. Thus strict gender roles, taboos about certain activities, seasonal observances, and so on were accepted and carefully followed—not simply out of fear of reprisal, but out of respect for what was viewed as the natural and proper order of things, as well as respect for the immense power of all natural things.

A Shasta man expected to pass his entire life within the area circumscribed by his own village and territory, and the territories of a few of the neighboring villages, often within a ten to twenty mile radius. This lack of curiosity about other lands and people, this lack of the Europeans' desire to travel and "see the world" was not, as condescending whites considered it, because of low intelligence and inherent laziness. True, the Shastan peoples, like other American Indians, had no idea of the full measure of lands and peoples

23

abroad. However, what kept the Shasta content within their apparently narrow world was a deep respect for and understanding of their own place in their ecosystem. "Ecosystem," however, does not really begin to touch upon their concept of a very real physical *and* metaphysical world, within which they had a certain place. From their point of view, by living within that place—and by respecting other creatures' and spirits' places—they contributed to the continuing harmony of their world.

Native Americans, as is reflected in their stories and mythology, did not see themselves as having dominion over the earth and its creatures. They were not ambitious to make their marks upon new lands or to change the world "for the better." That, to them, would not only have been a foolish waste of time, but would have demonstrated a lack of understanding and respect for the balance of nature, for the interdependence among all living things.

Naturally, such a value system left them unprepared for the actions of the whites. Not only did the Shastan peoples themselves not consider abusing the rights of the land and of the creatures who lived in it, but they could not conceive of anyone else wishing to do such a thing. They did not have the imagination (much less the experience) in purely psychological terms to help them grasp what the whites were capable of—what they were actually doing—until it was too late. Their lands were taken, their villages broken up, their families torn apart, and their social system undermined.

All this happened before ethnologists began recording the Shastan tribes' ancient culture. For that reason, much of what has been or can be written about these people is based on the accounts of single informants, on inferences that can be made from what the culture was like by the turn of this century, on limited archaeological excavations in the area, and on comparisons with other similar and neighboring tribes. The majority of this information concerns the largest of the four Shastan tribes, the Shastas. Given this, what might "home" for a pre-contact Shasta have been like?

The Village and Village Structures

Tchuar-xia [Little Moon] laughed as she sang and stamped her feet. The damp soil between her toes felt cool and smooth, and the umma [dwelling house] floor was beginning to harden, so the dust no longer rose in the air around them. As Tchuar-xia, her mother, her sister, and her sisters-in-law stamped their feet and sang, her grandmother sprinkled water from a carrying basket onto the fine dirt that had been sifted to form the building's floor.

Tchuar-xia looked above her at the smooth lines of the pine logs the men had peeled and placed to form the roof supports. The air inside the new umma smelled clean and fresh with the scent of pine and the cedar bark that she and the other women had wedged into the sides to line the earthen walls.

Smiling, Tchuar-xia stamped carefully around the sunken fire pit in the umma's center. "My brother's family will be warm in here this winter," she thought, "and I can come here to their fire to play with the babies and listen to Grandmother tell stories."

Villages were generally small, made up of a few families, sometimes even of a single (extended) family; thus most village populations ranged from fifteen to forty persons. A male would generally pass his entire life as a resident of the village of his birth. His wife usually would be chosen from the village of a neighboring Shastan band. So, while a woman might have a bit more uprooting, she too never lived far from familiar people and scenes, from the traditional lifestyle and ritual.

Most Shasta villages were located alongside rivers or streams, for the obvious conveniences. Each village "owned" the fishing rights to its portion of the river. The lands around the village, too, were recognized as the property of the villagers, and if outsiders from another village hunted, fished, or gathered food or materials within this territory, they might be assessed damages, determined by the chief of the area. Each family within the village also had its own recognized territory and first rights to its use. But although individuality and individual rights were respected, the sense of community was also strong. The meat from a large kill of deer, elk, or bear, for example, was shared equally with all members of the village. The hunter retained right to only the skin and legs, and he gave larger shares to any villagers who were old or infirm.

A typical Shasta village included one or more dwelling houses (*umma*), each occupied by one or more families; an assembly house (*okwaumma*) located near the center of the village; and a menstrual hut (*wapsahuumma*) located on the west side of the village. In addition, a larger village had a men's gathering place and sweathouse (*wukwu*) situated near the stream. In most villages, individual families also constructed their own smaller sweathouses, used by all members of the family.

In basic form, the umma and the okwaumma were similar to those of the northcoast Yurok and the neighboring Karuk. Construction began with the men of the village working together to excavate the interior of the rectangular structure to a depth of three to four feet. They then peeled oak, pine, or fir poles to make ridge and side supports and set them on forked posts to support the single-peaked board roof. The side walls were formed by piling dirt along the edge of the excavation to meet the roof. The men built end walls of planks and cut a doorway (facing the river) into one of the planks about three feet above ground. At the back of an umma they also constructed a lean-to kennel for the dogs, which families kept primarily for hunting.

At this point construction was taken over by the women. For the floor, the women sifted, dampened, and trampled the dirt until it was hard and smooth. They hung the doorway with a heavy mat woven from swamp tule. The social and practical center of the building, the round fireplace, was built by lining a hole with stones and cutting a smokehole into the roof above it.

There were, of course, differences between the umma and okwaumma buildings, each of which was suited to its specialized purpose. The dwelling house, generally about sixteen by twenty. feet, was excavated less deeply and its inside dirt walls were lined with rougher materials—cedar slabs, bark, or sometimes pine boards. Still, the Shasta family looked to their practical comfort. Insulation in the form of pine needles was carefully layered between the dirt and the wood, and the packed dirt floor was often covered by tule mats.

The interior of the umma was designed to minimize clutter, since ten to fifteen people might spend much of the winter in the dwelling. The living space itself extended to within one and one-half feet of the walls, at which place planks were set to form a short wall, creating individual storage bins. These were lined with woven maple leaf mats, which were waterproof to protect clothing, ornaments, and other personal possessions stored there. The family members rolled their animal hide bedding and tule-bundle or wooden block pillows against these half-walls.

At the entrance door to the umma, a sort of entry hall was formed by two walls, extending about three feet into the living area. The women used the corner nooks created by these walls to store cooking utensils, and it was here that the women of the family—the grandmother, wife, sisters, daughters, daughters-in-law—generally sat, backs to the fire, to pound acorns into the flour that was the family's staple food.

The village's largest building, the okwaumma, was planned by the village chief, constructed by other men in the village, and cleaned by the old women. The Shasta used their okwaumma as a sort of community hall, as did many California Indians, but not as a general sleeping or sweating quarters as, for example, did the Maidu to the south. Meetings and dances, both ceremonial and recreational, were held there, and gambling and games might take place in the okwaumma. Occasionally, if a family had more visitors than they had room to sleep in their umma, some might stay the night in the okwaumma. Considered the property of the chief, the assembly house went to his male heir upon the chief's death. If he had no male heirs, the labor and materials put into the building notwithstanding, the house was either burned or abandoned.

When building the okwaumma, the men dug an excavation to six or seven feet, and roughly twenty by twenty-seven feet in size. Outside, the okwaumma was plain, with earth-covered sides and roof. The inside walls, however, insulated in the same manner as in the umma, were lined with split boards rather than cedar slabs or bark, and the building's centerpost was often painted red and black. The end walls, too, were earth-sheltered, and the door could only be reached through a tunnel dug in the earth piled at the okwaumma's end.

The other important building, the wukwu, or men's sweathouse, was built on slightly different lines than were the umma and the okwaumma. Excavating deeply as they did with the assembly house, the men constructed an earth-sheltered building whose roof was only slightly raised above ground level. This roof they piled heavily with dirt and pine needles so that the resulting structure was almost airtight.

Large enough for fifteen to twenty men—all the men of an average-sized village—the wukwu was entered by means of a small hole cut into one of the plank interior walls at about waist height. In the ground just outside the hole were two stakes by which a man could pull himself out. The firepit was built at the east end of the building with a draft hole behind it but with no smokehole above it. When they wished, the men could close both the draft and the door holes by means of planks. The flooring in a wukwu was wooden, and the men used blocks of wood as pillows. This was a dry heat sweathouse, heated only by the wood fire.

For the village men, the wukwu was their club or lodgehouse. Women were not allowed in, and each man of the village had his own designated place to sleep. The men gathered there to work or lounge, perhaps crafting knives, bows, or arrows as they talked about an upcoming hunt. They also, of course, gathered in the wukwu to sweat for both health and ritual purification. In addition,

A Shasta sweathouse. Courtesy of Siskiyou County Historical Society.

in some villages, unmarried men and boys from the age of ten or twelve upwards slept in the sweathouse. While the wukwu, like the assembly house, was also considered the property of the chief, this building continued to be used upon his death, and proprietorship passed to the new chief.

In a village too small and poor to construct a wukwu, each family would at least build a small family sweathouse. Even in larger villages that had men's sweathouses, individual families generally had their own for the use of family members, especially for women's ritual cleansing after menstruation, childbirth, and widowhood, as well as for their own daily sweating to ensure health. These small sweathouses, whose construction was generally the job of the women, were dome-shaped and made from pliant willow poles, showing the influence of northeast tribal culture. The women bent these poles and covered them with pine bark and animal skins. These were steam sudatories, water being thrown onto hot rocks piled inside the hut. Entrance was through a small, ground-level hole which usually faced east.

The Sweathouse: A Reminiscence by Winnie Nelson

They built the sweathouse away from the house and they put rocks in a fire outside the sweathouse. Then they brought the rocks inside the sweathouse and piled them up. The sweathouse was dome shaped and was made of willow poles covered with canvas hides or whatever they had to keep the heat in. And then they would take a basket of water and put it on the inside and while they took their sweatbath the water was getting warm. If it started to get cool in the sweathouse they would throw water on the rocks to get more steam. Four or five, maybe six people could get in there. If it got too hot you could lift the flap and stick your head out. I can remember when I was a little girl. Oh—I got so hot I always had to stick my head out. The rest of the body was in the sweathouse. Sometimes they would go to the creek and bathe after a sweatbath but most of the time they had warm water in there in the Indian baskets and they would wash themselves with that warm water. A lot of people say the Indians always jumped in a creek or took a cold bath after coming out of the sweathouse but they didn't always. Some took warm baths. Of course after a funeral or something like that...they would all go and take baths in the creek or river. I can remember when I was a little girl they used to make me go to the creek and take a bath the first thing in the morning. Every morning that's what they did with us. We didn't swim. We would get in right quick: If you get in quick you don't feel the cold.[*]

The final building in the village, the wapsahuumma, or menstrual hut, was always built entirely by the women. Always located on the west, or dark (i. e., sunset), side of the village, at least eight to ten feet from the nearest dwelling house, it was similar in plan to the dwelling house, though much smaller and poorer. In the Shasta Valley, some villages did build their wapsahuumma on a slightly different plan, as a double lean-to, bark covered, and with

---

* Winnie Nelson, who was half-Shasta, was born in Siskiyou County in the 1880s. This account, from a tape transcription published in Pat Martin, "The Shasta," in the 1971 *Siskiyou Pioneer*, is reprinted courtesy of the Siskiyou County Historical Society.

a dirt-covered roof, but still the women expended little care on this building.

In all villages, though, despite its less careful or elaborate construction, the wapsahuumma was of vital importance. Like most California Indians, the Shastan people believed that a menstruating woman was full of great powers, and therefore potentially dangerous both to others and to herself. Thus the taboos governing her behavior were very strict. The wapsahuumma was essential to provide her a safe place to stay well away from the rest of her villagers, particularly the hunters, whose luck she could spoil. The menstrual hut was also used for childbirth and for the mother and child's postnatal seclusion period (usually one month).

Because of their established villages with permanent structures, the Shastan tribes are not considered nomadic. The villages, however, were the people's home primarily during the cold winter months, though old people often resided there year-round. During the warmer months, unneeded tools, ornaments, clothing, and household items would also be left behind in the ummas.

The Shasta left their villages to follow their food sources during the moderate months, still, however, staying pretty much within their recognized territories. In the spring and summer, families moved into roofless willow and brush shelters near prime root- and plant-gathering and fishing areas; and in the early fall, during the acorn-gathering season, families moved to individual-family pine or cedar bark shelters near the oak groves. In the late fall, the families camped out in the forested mountains for the big hunts, finally returning by early winter, well-laden for the upcoming lean months, to the village and their homes.

Shasta baskets. Courtesy of Fort Jones Museum.

Food

The Shasta were a hunting and gathering culture, living off the considerable bounty their lands provided them. Nuts and other plant foods, fish, and game all formed part of their diet, with acorn, deer meat, and salmon being the dietary staples. Women gathered and dug plant foods, though both sexes shared the task of acorn gathering, with the men shaking down the acorns and the women gathering them into carrying baskets. Both sexes also gathered pine nuts and hazelnuts. Fishing was primarily a male activity, though the women did some basket-fishing and helped in the fish drives. Men had almost sole responsibility for the hunting, including manufacturing the weapons.

Gathering

Gwatintin [Already Round One] looked down at his sister and his girl-cousins from his perch in the branches of the hatukihu *[black oak tree]. Tchuar-xia's carrying basket was only half full, and she called up to her brother.*

"Stop daydreaming, Gwatintin!" she called. "We need more acorns!"

Gwatintin stood up on the branch, balancing himself by holding onto the next branch overhead. Flexing his knees, he bounced up and down, and a light rain of acorns fell to the ground. He laughed as the little girls ran out from under the tree, holding their arms over their heads.

"Gwatintin! Don't tease you sisters. Remember that you are not a sukwahia *[little boy] any more!" From her spot in the shade of a neighboring tree, his* ammuhi's *[maternal grandmother's] hands were poised over the acorns she was sorting in her lap.*

The Shasta's plant food diet was varied. Acorns (black oak were preferred) were a dietary staple, as they were with most neighboring tribes. The women's preparation of the acorns was a lengthy process, involving first hulling and drying the meats, pounding them to meal in a bottomless mortar basket on a flat stone, and then winnowing and sifting the meal. The resultant fine meal was then leached repeatedly with warm water through a sieve of pine needles and sand to remove the bitterness. After leaching, the sweet acorn paste was ready for final cooking into a mush or soup, or, if the harvest had been plentiful, the dough might be dried and saved in storage baskets. For soup, which was prepared in a cooking basket, the women stirred the acorn paste into water they had first brought to boiling by dropping in stones heated in the fire.

The women gathered other plant foods for their village: manzanita berries (which were also used to make cider), blackberries, elderberries, gooseberries, thimbleberries (some eaten fresh, some dried for mixing with other foods); roots and bulbs (often boiled or roasted); and wild greens (including wild varieties of parsley, celery, and rhubarb). The women used sharpened, forked sticks to dig for roots and bulbs. In some areas, the people broadcast seeds, and many Shastan bands practiced controlled burning of areas to clear out undergrowth and encourage the growth of particular plants.

In addition to the plant foods dug and gathered, the women and children collected grasshoppers, crickets, and yellow jacket larvae, which they would later dry and pound into a meal to mix with grass seeds. At the rivers the women and children dove for mussels and crawfish. These they often dried in the sun and stored for the winter. Later they would prepare the shellfish for eating by boiling them.

Fishing

Gwatintin held his breath as his father, holding a pinch of tobacco and herbs between his thumb and forefinger, spoke. "I give this to you, first kitar *[salmon], and I ask that you give to me many fish to feed my family. I come to you clean, and have done nothing wrong. Give me many fish!"*

He moved his fingers as he called out, and Gwatintin watched the powder drift in the air and come to rest on the smooth surface of the little pool. He remembered coming to this spot, and others like it, with his father earlier that summer. They had carefully replaced the piled rocks around the edges of the creek that had washed away over the winter and spring, reforming little pools of smooth, still water within the course of the rapids. "The salmon will rest here, on their journey upriver," his father had explained. Then they had rebuilt the fishing platform at the bank's edge that his father now stood upon, and the salmon callers had sung prayers to the earth mother for the salmon's safe return upstream.

Now it was summer, the salmon had begun their run, and Gwatintin's father, who owned the fishing rights to this stretch of Wasudigwa *[the Klamath River], had come to call the salmon and*

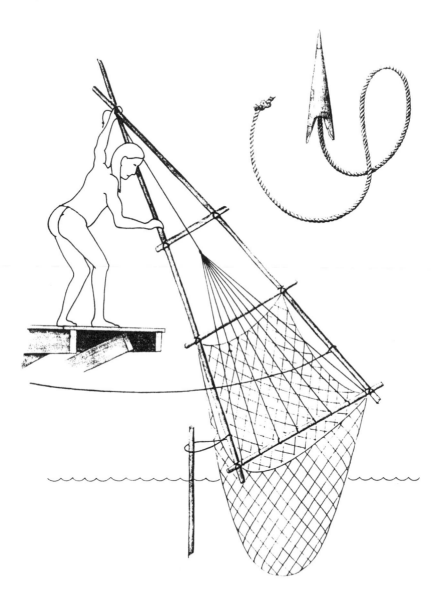

Fishing net. Fish hook.

remind them of the tribe's respect and need for them before fishing began.

Although anthropologists' accounts of the procedures differ, contemporary Shasta state that salmon calling rituals were (and are) an important and traditional observance. Another form of salmon ritual involved allowing the first salmon that passed to continue unharmed on its way upstream. The first fish caught after that had to be cleaned and hung to dry. No further salmon might be eaten until that second salmon had dried and been shared among all the men who were fishing in that area. Still another group of Shastas tied their ritual to the neighboring Karuk tribe's White Deerskin Dance, allowing fishing and drying of the salmon, but holding off eating the fish until the dance had been performed. Some of the Shastan tribes also had taboos regarding fishermen's behavior, and about cooking and eating the salmon catch. For example, men were to remain celibate during net fishing; cooking done by a menstruating woman was thought to ruin the fishing; and puberty-aged youth were not allowed to eat of the first salmon run's catch. Similar rituals and taboos may also have been connected with other catches—including trout, steelhead, and sucker fish.

The Shasta carried out the actual fishing process itself using a variety of methods: weirs and basket traps, spears, drives, hooks and lines, and nets. Weirs, or fish dams, were constructed of stakes and poles, secured by grape vines, and interlaid in most places with brush weighted down with stones. In the scattered openings, the men placed long, willow fish traps. Three known locations of such weirs were in shallow, gravelly spots at the mouth of the Shasta River, at the Scott River, and at Happy Camp. Although one or two men held rights to each weir, anyone might spear fish from the dams.

Men also built platforms out from the banks of a stream where the eddy was strong for net fishing. These platforms, rebuilt after spring floods, were also "rededicated" each year in a ritual. The large nets used for platform fishing were constructed with a triangular draw top and a long handle, so that the fisherman might stand upright and place his net in the stream. When the fisherman felt the strings of the net pulled by the passage of fish into the net, he lifted the net out, and the top of the net was drawn closed by the weight of the fish.

The floating drive, perhaps practiced only by the Klamath River Shasta, involved the women in the fishing. Lying on rough log rafts in the river, the women thrashed the water with branches. Floating downstream as they beat the water, the women drove the frightened fish into a barrier of men, standing shoulder to shoulder and wielding spears. Taboos decreed that the people remain at the river to eat—that same day—all the fish caught in this way. In other Shasta tribes, men and women waded in the stream, beating the surface of the water, to drive the fish into a weir or trap.

When ritual or taboos did not otherwise decree, the Shasta often dried and smoked the fish they caught, then stored it in baskets (sometimes leaf-lined), either in slices or in a powder form the women made by rubbing the dried fish between their palms. If they were going to eat the fish fresh, they roasted it over an open fire.

Hunting

Tchuar-xia shivered with excitement and stamped her feet against the snowy ground, more because she just couldn't stand still than because of the cold. Her deerskin hakuai *[leggings] and* hanniteema *[shirt] kept her body warm, and her winter* hachah *[moccasins] were fur-lined.*

But her mind and body still tingled with the excitement of the kustehempik *[dancing] and* katsnik *[singing] that had gone on late into the night before, as the people prayed and readied themselves for the big* aro *[deer] hunt of the winter's first* kau *[snow]. For this hunt, everyone in the village took part, not just the men, and Tchuar-xia loved running through the snow-crusted oak forest.*

Snowshoes.

In a few years she would be old enough to wear the miri *[snowshoes] and carry the club of the hunters, and then she would share the responsibility of feeding the family, of getting fresh venison for children and old people. But for today, she could walk through the beauty of the snowy hills, helping to spot the deer trails the hunters would follow. And today, on such a beautiful morning, that was enough.*

Rituals, again designed to reinforce the balance and harmony of the Shasta's interaction with the other creatures of the earth, were as much a part of hunting as of fishing. The rituals themselves varied with the game involved, the season, and even the hunter's own age. A bear hunt, for example, was preceded by a five-day ritual sweat and an actual war dance. Sexual continence was usually practiced before a hunt, and a man might not hunt during his wife's menstrual period. Both the hunter himself and his weapons were purified over smoke, offerings of eagle down and/or tobacco might be made, and the hunter might fast for a period before going hunting. In almost all cases, the hunter would perform a ritual sweat and prayer before his hunt. After a successful hunt, prayers for the spirit of the animal would again be offered. A youth who made his first kill was also subject to certain taboos, such as not eating of the meat. In some groups the boy's father ritually whipped the successful new hunter with his bowstring.

Deer, the primary game food, was hunted almost year-round, though not during the deer's late fall mating season. The hunting methods themselves were varied and generally involved male hunters only, the exception being the big winter hunt after the first snow. At this time, the entire village would follow the deer trails into the live oak stands, where the deer wintered, for a big winter kill.

The Shasta men also hunted deer using snares, nets, and traps across the deer's trails and near their licks, especially in the spring. Stalking was a common technique, and the hunter had several variations of deerskin disguises to wear for the different seasons. In summer, for example, he would don a stuffed deerhead with mink-fur covered horns to approximate the velvet antlers the deer have at that time.

Sometimes the deer were driven into traps, water, or snares and then clubbed or shot with arrows. In the late autumn, the Shasta used fire to drive the deer and to clear out the forest's underbrush. At this time of year, when the deer were fat and putting on their heavier coats, a very fast man who had powerful hunting magic might also run down or drive the deer himself. If he was driving the deer, the hunter would call out "Peu, peu, peu" and beat the brush with a willow or hazel stick as he ran. Other hunters would lie in wait, listening to the runner's call. When the deer ran past, they would shoot it. After the deer was butchered, the runner would receive the head and skin, but the other hunters would take the meat. No deer were hunted after the late fall drives, however, because that period began their mating season. The hunters used similar techniques for taking antelope and elk, though the latter were hunted primarily in winter, and the hunters, wearing snow-shoes, ran them down.

Bears, valued for their fat, meat, and warm pelts, were generally attacked in their dens. Just outside the den, the hunters drove sharp-pointed stakes into the ground. Then they stood before the den and talked to the bear and called him to come outside. When the bear emerged from his den and became entangled in the stakes, the hunters shot him under the neck.

The Shasta hunted the abundant small game and birds in their area using traps, nets, clubs, bows and arrows, nooses, and snares. The smaller game included rabbits, beavers, minks, squirrels, and other small mammals, and quail.

The Shasta kept dogs for use in hunting, chiefly on the drives. The men trained their hunting dogs carefully for the jobs, singing the "Blowfly Song" and the "Grizzly Song" to them so that the animals' scent might be keen and their courage high.

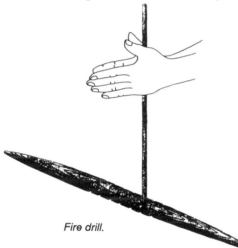

Fire drill.

Among all the Shastan tribes, food, whether gathered, fished, or hunted, was distributed among the families of the village, no matter who had garnered it. No one received a greater share than another, though the best parts of the game were traditionally given to the old people, with the hunter cutting up the meat and his wife distributing it. Those who transgressed against this communal spirit and acted in a stingy or selfish fashion were shunned, though even they were given a share of the food that others had obtained.

The meat itself was cooked in a variety of ways. A large portion was smoked and dried, to be later eaten as jerky or boiled in water, sometimes as an addition to acorn soup. Some of the dried meat might also be pounded into powder form for easier storage and portability for traveling. Fresh meat was boiled, roasted, or rolled in leaves and baked in an earth oven. Marrow, bones, stomach, intestines—all parts of the animals were prepared and used.

The entire food gathering cycle was just that—a cycle, following the earth's own rhythms, changing with each season. Spring meant the onset of grizzly hunting, as the big bears awakened, and the time to gather tender early greens and to dive for mussels. As warm summer approached, the people moved to brush shelters near their fishing spots. Acorns ripened in early fall, and while women gathered and cached acorns in the hills, men hunted deer. At this time all of the villagers but the elderly camped in the hills, with the older people remaining behind in the permanent homes, perhaps mending tools, baskets, and clothing.

Later in the fall, and higher in the mountains, the hunters held their last big deer drive of the season, and everyone was busy cutting and drying the deer meat, pounding the bones into a coarse meal for winter soups, and storing it all in large baskets, all of which would be evenly distributed among the people before they trekked back to the village. Also, after the hunt was completed, the people returned to collect the acorns they had gathered earlier in the fall. These all had to be hulled, cracked, dried, ground, and leached to meal for storage. This coincided with the deer's mating season, so while the women were busy with the acorn preparation, the men hunted small game and fished, and everyone worked at other tasks—wood gathering, tanning hides, making and repairing winter clothing and snowshoes—to make ready for the onset of winter.

With winter's first snow came the big community deer hunt, and then individual elk and deer hunts, to provide the villagers with fresh meat as other supplies grew lower. This was the time for visiting neighboring villages if the weather permitted, storytelling, craft work, and playing games, as people waited for spring.

Appearance, Clothing, Ornamentation

"Be still, kiyaha *[little girl]. Stop moving your head!"*

Tchuar-xia turned back to her brother's tarichi *[wife] and held her head still as the young woman finished painting the red stripes on Tchuar-xia's cheeks.*

"There!" she said. "Now go off while I finish."

Tchuar-xia walked just outside the brush shelter and stood beside the large burden baskets. She peered inside and saw they were already filled with ground acorn meal to carry to the dance at the village in the next valley. Looking up again, she watched her brother's wife comb her long hair with the porcupine-quill brush, wrap the hair into two braids, and finally tie each with mink skin strips sewn with red woodpecker feathers. When she then set the round atsik *[basket cap] on her head, Tchuar-xia thought how pretty her oldest brother's wife was. The dentalium and mussel shell beaded* hahyi *[apron] the young woman wore made a soft rustling sound as she bent to tie on the painted and fancy-stitched moccasins that were saved for dances.*

Tchuar-xia's own feet fidgeted with impatience as she waited for the rest of the village women—her mother, older sister, sister-in-law, four aunts, and her old grandmother—to announce they were ready. She looked across from the brush shelters toward the river, where the men, including her two oldest brothers, were gathered. Young cousins, nieces, and nephews ran about shouting, but Tchuar-xia noticed that Gwatintin, the brother only three years older than she, stood silently at the edge of the men's group.

The little girl sighed. Lately Gwatintin spent more time with the men than he used to, and today, Tchuar-xia noticed, her youngest brother wore his hair tied up on his head like her father and the other men did and had painted red and black designs down his arms.

Tchuar-xia turned away, then suddenly reached out and caught one of her young cousins as he ran by. She swung the sukwahia *[little boy] in a circle, laughing with him. It was a wonderful day to go to a dance.*

Early anthropologist Stephen Powers ([1877] 1976, 243-44)—who is not known for objectivity or open-mindedness—describes the Shastas of the 1870s as small-boned and fine-featured, yet (in particular reference to the women) vigorous and strong. Lieutenant G. H. Emmons, during an exploratory expedition in 1841, commented on the Shasta as "a fine looking race, being better proportioned than those more to the northward, and their features more regular" (Wilkes 1845, 5: 239). H. H. Bancroft (1883, 1:328-29) cites various travelers of the mid-1800s who described the aboriginal people of this area as "well grown and muscular," and having "smooth hazel skins," and "almond shaped eyes, sometimes of a hazel color." It is known that the Shasta considered a broad and square face the ideal, and an infant's forehead and/or chin might be wrapped and flattened with a beaded pad when the child was in the cradleboard in order to achieve the proper proportions.

Like other tribes of the area, the Shasta dressed primarily in buckskin clothing. But beaver, otter, fox, raccoon, and squirrel skins might also be used, especially for warmer winter clothing such as robes and shawls, and for men's caps. Both men and women tanned the skins, first scraping off the hair, then softening the skins by soaking them with a paste made of deer brains, grass, and moss.

The garments were generally sewn by the women, and varied according to the age and gender of the wearer and, of course, the season and activity. Daily wear for both boys and girls was often nothing more than breechclouts. A knee-length shirt and moccasins might be added in cold weather or for visiting.

Apron of pine nuts, woven Bear grass and ferns, and leather. Courtesy of Fort Jones Museum.

In warm weather, men might wear nothing at all, a

breechclout, or a buckskin draped about the hips. In cooler weather and for dress occasions, a shirt, leggings, and moccasins were added. Dress moccasins were not only decorated with painted seams and fancy stitching, but were also made without soles. In addition, a raccoon or fox skin robe, with hair and tail left on, might be worn.

Buckskin shirt, skirt, and apron made by Carrie Wicks, a Scott Valley Shasta, circa 1925. Courtesy of Bess and Tom Webster.

Women's dress included the traditional (to most Northern California tribes) doubled deerskin skirt. The underskirt was often a wrap of plain buckskin which met at the back, and the overskirt, which met (or almost met) at the front, was ornamented with or composed entirely of deep fringe. This fringe was commonly decorated with shells, pine nuts, or beaded grasswork. Often a long and narrow front apron of fringe strips, decorated with nuts, seeds, shells, or braided grass, was also worn. Women always wore a close-fitting woven basket cap, sometimes decorated with interwoven designs. In cool weather or for visiting, women might also wear a fringed shirt (similar to the men's) or perhaps a length of buckskin wrapped around the chest under the arms and hanging to the waist.

In winter weather—which can be bitterly cold in the Siskiyous—men, women, and children wrapped themselves with robes

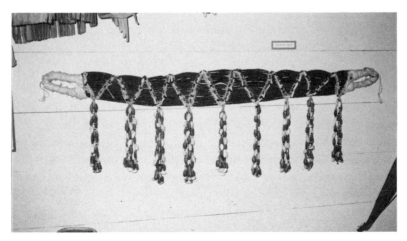

Braided horsehair and beads belt. Courtesy of Fort Jones Museum.

of fox or raccoon skins. The women oiled their moccasins with fish oil, and the men oiled theirs with bear, deer, or wildcat oil to keep the leather supple and waterproof. Accounts vary as to the moccasins the Shastan people wore. Some anthropologists claim that sole-less moccasins were the only type of footwear worn until the full moccasin was introduced by tribes from the east. Snowshoes,

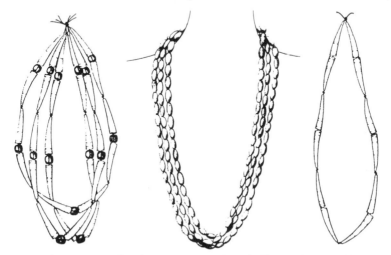

a. Dentalium shell and trade bead necklace; b. Pine nut bead necklace; c. Dentalium currency string.

made of hazelwood and cross-lashed with rope and deer hide, might also be worn if necessary.

Both sexes wore ornamental necklaces, pierced-ear and -nose decorations, and head- and wristbands fashioned from feathers (especially the highly prized yellowhammer feathers and wood-pecker scalps), as well as from pine nuts, dentalia, mussel, and other shells. These ornamental materials were often obtained by trade, and those coming from other areas were highly prized. For dress occasions, women wore belts woven of hair and deerskin strips, beaded or decorated with porcupine-quill work. They might also dress their hair with feathers and beads. Men wore narrow headbands decorated with feathers or whole woodpecker scalps with the bills left on.

Accounts on the use of body paints conflict. Some (e. g., Dixon) say paint was little used except in healing and war ceremonies. Others (e. g., Holt and Curtis) cite informants who mention the use of paint by both sexes for special occasions. These paints, com-pounded from marrow, grease, and various natural pigments, were black, white, red, and yellow. Each individual painted his or her own design on face and arms. Young girls (prepubescent) were limited to having each cheek painted with three or four red stripes.

Also connected to puberty was chin tattooing for females, a cultural tradition the Shasta shared with many other California tribes. When a girl was about ten or eleven, an old woman in the village tattooed several parallel stripes across the girl's chin, using a sharp obsidian flake. No girl wanted to forego this ritual because untattooed women were mocked and considered unattractive, and risked being teased and called "Leather-face" by members of other villages.

Travel

Gwatintin held up a string of kaqitik [dentalium shells] in the light. Their milky whiteness shone, and he thought that they would

surely buy a fine basket of the tan oak acorns that his kimpiwa
*[oldest brother] planned to bring back for the family. The boy held
the string to his arm, mimicking the action of his* ata *[father], who
stood beside him measuring each strand by holding one end in his
palm and stretching the string along the inside of his arm, against
the measurement* kipti *[tattoos] traced on his skin.*

*The hide pack at Gwatintin's feet was almost full of kaqitik,
softly tanned buckskin hides, and pine nuts. Looking up, he saw his
brother touch his tongue to a fine obsidian* hatsirai *[knife] as the
sunlight glinted off its black surface.*

In addition to close ties between the family and village unit, the
Shastan people maintained close trading and visiting ties between
bands within the tribe. Indeed, this closeness, connected in part to
the marriage process [discussed later], has helped to ensure the
survival of the Shasta as a people. It must be noted that even with
the travel to visit other tribes, Karuk or Wintu, for example, the
Shasta stayed comparatively close to home and their land.

The most common reason for travel was hunting and gathering.
For a hunt, men might travel as far as fifteen or twenty miles from
their village, being careful, however, not to trespass on the hunting
grounds of another village. The same was true of acorn gathering:
The group might range several miles from the winter village, but
would only cover that territory traditionally deemed theirs.

Shasta men also traveled to the lava beds in the east, on the edge
of Modoc territory, to obtain obsidian for knives and arrowheads.
Among some groups, a trip of this sort was part of a youth's
puberty rite, since it involved travel of some distance as well as
danger of attack by the Modoc.

Warfare was also a reason for travel, though, as mentioned
earlier, the Shasta were not an especially warlike group. A few
accounts (Powers, Silver, Kroeber) mention intermittent but in-
tense feuds between the Shasta Valley and Scott Valley bands,
though other accounts do not mention this. The Modoc, however,

according to all accounts, were traditional enemies who raided Shasta villages and took women and children as slaves. The Shasta retaliated against them, as well as occasionally against the Wintu for trespassing on hunting rights. Some anthropologists and historians have theorized that intratribal and especially intertribal fighting only became common as the tribes were crowded closer and closer, and resources became scarcer due to increasing white incursion.

Before men went to war, they held ritual dances, singing, and sweat ceremonies. They took bows and arrows on their raids, and they often wore stick and elkhide armor for protection. During a raid, the Shasta warriors often burned the enemy's village (though not in an intratribal feud), and then freed the Shasta women and/or children who had been taken prisoner (the reason for the raid). A victory dance appears to have been uncommon after a war raid, and only a few accounts mention the Shasta taking prisoners or slaves.

More frequently than for war or raids, the Shasta traveled to the villages of other tribes to trade for goods not manufactured by the Shasta or available in their area. Bringing their goods in hide packs or large carrying baskets, the Shasta traded buckskins, obsidian, and the commonly-used currency of the area, strings of dentalium shells, to the Wintu in exchange for clamshell beads and acorns. Little trade was carried on with the Modoc or Klamath Lake tribes to the east, but heavy trading went on between the Shasta and the coastal tribes to the west and the Oregon groups around the Rogue River. Again, the currency was strings of dentalium shells, sometimes carved and incised, and often measured against tattoo marks along the inside of a man's arm. Barter was also common. With their northern neighbors, the Shasta most often traded acorn paste for dentalium. With the Karuk, Hupa, and Yurok, the Shasta traded obsidian blades, juniper beads, pine nuts, and buckskins; in return they received dentalia, baskets, various shells and beads, and certain kinds of acorns not available in Shasta territories. The Shasta traded for, or occasionally made, canoes, but used them less commonly than did the Yurok and Karuk toward the coast.

Short-range travel between villages within each tribe's territory was common. The Shasta made frequent trips between villages, almost always on foot, to arrange marriages, to trade, to celebrate such important rituals as girls' puberty ceremonies and shaman initiations, and to just visit and enjoy a chance to gossip, tell stories, gamble, and play games.

If a group were to travel some distance, they brought with them some of their traditional and specialized food as a gift for their hosts: maybe antelope meat from Shasta Valley, specialized bulbs from Scott Valley, or perhaps salmon and pine nuts from the bands on the Klamath River. Visitors were always welcomed and fed when they arrived and were given gifts at departure.

Games

Outside, the snow flurries blew, but inside, in the warmth of the umma, the children crowded around the players. Tchuar-xia's face was flushed, only partly from the warmth of the fire, as she leaned forward.

Holding the stick in her hand and keeping her arm straight, she moved the game piece slowly and evenly back and forth at her side. Then, in one quick and sweeping motion, she swung the stick forward so that the attached string of bone disks flew up into the air above the point of the stick. As the disks fell, she caught five on the tip of the stick, but the important last disk, the eye of the moon, grazed the point and slipped down loosely to the end of the string.

"Acha [five]! Only acha!" cried Gwatintin. "You'll never catch the eye! Do you want wugi *[winter] to last forever? Let me try— let me!"*

The Shasta, both children and adults, played many games, some of which, including the men's and women's gambling games, were quite serious and attended by elaborate rituals and taboos. Some, like the above-mentioned version of the ring and pin game, were played both for amusement and with some ritual significance, and others were played simply for amusement.

The gambling games were similar to games played by many tribes across the Americas. Men and women each had their own forms of gambling games, the men's similar to the grass games played by the Maidu and other tribes of Central California, and the women's like those of the Hupa women.

These adult gambling games could only be played outside the village group and were regarded as both a form of amusement and as serious, ritual-bound activity. During the course of play, everyone—not just players—was subject to dietary restrictions and had to observe celebacy. Play might continue for two or three days straight, though seldom longer since players were not allowed to sleep. The losing side might even have its shaman bewitch their opponents to make them sleepy.

Ketapiq, the men's gambling game, was a ritual-governed guessing game which used painted sticks as counters. Making the gaming sticks themselves involved a good bit of ceremony. In preparation for making the sticks, which was generally a two-man task, the men practiced sexual continence for five days. The sticks were then made during a journey the men took into a sacred place of power in the mountains. Throughout the journey and the construction of the sticks, the men sang, prayed, and observed certain dietary restrictions. Even after their return with the finished and painted sticks, the men were subject to another five days of continence and ritual bathing. The sticks were then bound together with a cord—often with a lucky charm, such as a red stone, tucked alongside—and carefully put away until they could be used.

The game itself involved two players. Each player had one or more bundles of fifteen or twenty painted spindle-shaped sticks, called *a'nninai*, along with two unpainted sticks called *ak*. Actual play was similar to that in games still played today by many Native American tribes. The two players sat facing each other. The first player took up one of his marked and one of his unmarked sticks

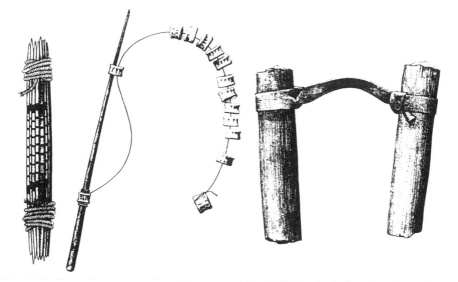

a. Men's gambling sticks; b. Salmon vertebrae and stick game; c. Women's kiratik game pieces.

and rolled each in a bunch of dried grass so that the player opposite could not see the markings. Then, as he sang his personal gambling song, he quickly shuffled the two bunches and then challenged his opponent to guess which bundle contained the marked stick. A correct guess won one of the painted sticks and passed the deal to the opponent. The first player to get all his opponent's sticks won. This was a public game, avidly watched by both players' families and neighbors. During the course of play, observers were also active singing, shouting encouragement, and placing bets.

The women's gambling game, *ku'ig*, was a similar guessing game using usually fifty or sixty painted and peeled willow sticks. These sticks were all painted alike except for one, and the object of the game was for one player to guess which bundle held the opponent's odd stick.

Also having ritual elements, but played more for amusement by both adults and children, was the ring and pin game. This game was generally played in winter to hasten the waning of the moon. The game piece consisted of a stick, about twelve to fifteen inches long, to which was attached a string of twelve salmon vertebrae (representing the twelve moons). The players tried to catch the vertebrae on the pointed end of the stick, with the last vertebrae, called the "eye of the moon," being the most important. A similar purpose was served by the children's string games (similar to cat's cradle), which were played to hurry the waxing of the moon.

The Shasta enjoyed playing physical games, including wrestling, shooting contests, races, spear throwing, and occasional circle dances (though most dances were connected with ritual observances). In addition, the women played *kiratik*, a form of shinny similar to that played by Maidu, Klamath, and Hupa tribes. Kiratik was a team sport, with two groups of four to ten on each side. Teams scored a goal by tossing a pair of short sticks, loosely tied together at the ends, over a goal at their team's end of the playing field. The players tried to keep the paired game sticks in the air, tossing them by means of throwing-sticks.

Storytelling was another primary form of amusement and was similarly connected with ritual and belief. Narrative tales of actual incidents might be told at any time, both to entertain and to teach the children (and remind the adult listeners) about family or tribal history and about approved conduct.

Sacred myths were told only during winter; some groups believed that telling the myths in summer, or even spring, might offend or actually bring rattlesnakes. Most storytelling was done in the evening by the old people, a certain old woman in the village frequently serving as resident storyteller. As the old woman told the story, the children often repeated it after her, line by line. At the end of the storytelling, the old woman would run her fingers down each child's back, pressing on certain vertebrae and, citing a corresponding animal, offer injunctions for strength (the grizzly bear), courage (the panther), industry, and other attributes.

Marriage

Gwatintin watched his older brother sorting the treasure. His arutsi [father's brother] had brought four new woodpecker scalps to add to the growing collection, and Gwatintin could see in his imagination the shimmering wrist and head bands they might become.

But of course he wouldn't really get to see what became of all the woodpecker scalps, nor of the large unstrung dentalium shells, nor the soft deerskins now piled on the tule mat in front of his brother. These treasures would go to pay the bride price for his brother's new wife.

"All of this must go?" Gwatintin couldn't help asking.

His brother laughed. "Our ata [father] says she is quiet and a good worker. She'll be a good wife, and these skins and shells mean our children will also be of great worth." He smiled. "Soon it'll be the marriage moon, and I've almost got the full bride price—so you'll see her for yourself. You must make her welcome in our umma, annu'iyawa [youngest brother]."

Among the Shastan tribes, marriage was arranged by means of bride purchase. Sometimes, in wealthy families, children might be promised to one another when quite young, and part or all of the bride price paid at that time. In other cases, marriages were generally arranged between residents of far off villages, since people within the village or even neighboring villages were often one's relations. The young man and woman might or might not know one another. Their wishes (particularly those of the young woman) were not usually of primary importance.

Contemporary Shasta describe a "marriage wheel," a practice decreed by Waka, the Great Spirit. This involved a careful accounting of genealogical lines, and an arranging of marriages by "trainers," who made sure both that individual bands did not intermarry too closely and that the connections among the Shasta bands would remain strong.

Sometimes a man's father took care of the actual negotiating with the bride's parents, though more often an intermediary, perhaps the "trainer," handled negotiations. During negotiations, both sides involved in arranging a marriage between their children were eager to agree to the highest possible bride price, since the worth of the couple's children (a sum used in determining blood-money payment for any injustices or crimes committed against a person) would be based upon the price paid for their mother. An average bride purchase might include dentalium shells, animal skins, woodpecker and yellowhammer scalps and feathers, and strings of beads.

Once a bride price had been agreed upon, the young man set about collecting the treasure, with his relatives contributing as much as they could. Accumulating the treasure might take a year, and a contemporary Shasta account states that marriages might only be arranged and finalized during the harvest moon each year, with arrangement taking place one year and the new couple being presented the next year.

After a couple married, they moved to the young man's village, often sharing the family umma at first, though they might build their own later. When the bride first came to her new home, she and her family members arrived dressed in their best. After a feast, the bride's family returned to its own village, though they would leave behind their dress clothes and ornaments as gifts. After three or four months of marriage, the new couple went on a one- or two-week visit to the bride's family, taking gifts with them. Only at the end of this visit was the marriage ceremony completed.

If a young man's family was very poor, he did have an option open to him. He might offer himself as a sort of indentured son-in-law to his would-be bride's family. He would agree to live permanently with the bride's family, and he would work for the bride's father, hunting, fishing, etc., until he had earned the agreed-upon bride price. If a young man were, for example, known to be a very fine hunter, he would have a good chance of striking such a bargain.

Crafts

Gwatintin ran into the umma. After the glare off the snow outside, the smoky darkness of the dwelling house made his eyes water. He stood for a moment, waiting for his eyes to adjust. The air was warm and slightly musty with the smell of dried foods and hides stored in the shelves along the sides, and of the women sitting by the fire rolling hemp for fish lines. As Gwatintin stood in the umma's entrance, the women burst into laughter at the closing line of the Quatak *[Coyote] story Grandmother had just told.*

The boy walked up to his grandmother. "I need a piece of the dried kitar *[salmon], Grandmother."*

"You are always hungry, Gwatintin," said his brother's new wife from where she sat beside her mother-in-law, winding the completed hemp cord around the shuttle.

Tchuar-xia laughed. "You should go help our father."

Gwatintin ignored them both. "My brother's making new pipes, Grandmother, and we need the salmon grubs to work for us."

His old grandmother eased herself up from the bearskin blanket on which she was sitting, went to one of the storage baskets, and drew out a large piece of dried salmon. She pointed to the series of little holes across one side of the meat. "There are your little workers." As the boy turned to go, she reminded him, "Don't waste the meat when you've finished setting the pipes!"

He answered respectfully, but when Gwatintin had climbed through the low umma door, he kicked sharply at the snow along the path back to the wukwu *[men's house] where the men were working. Holding the piece of salmon carefully as he walked along, he thought, "They all speak to me like I'm still a child!"*

Once the newly married couple had returned to the husband's village and settled into his father's or their own umma, they busied themselves with the many tasks day-to-day life required of every member of the community. In addition to obtaining and preparing food and clothing, which everyone worked on, the men spent time constructing tools and weapons. Basketry and weaving were some of the women's other duties. Children helped with tasks, too, learning the skills they would practice as adults.

In manufacturing their tools and

Obsidian arrowheads. Obsidian knife blades.   inches

weapons, the Shasta made use of stone, obsidian, bone, and the various hard and soft woods available. They also used animal leathers, wild hemp, and certain grasses for netting and lashing. While the Shasta did not use stone mortars (and, in fact, held that the occasional mortar left in their territory by another group had mysterious powers), they made and used stone pestles, shallow bowls or platters (soapstone was usually used for these), and pipe-tips. They used obsidian extensively for arrowheads, blades, and hide scrapers. Because of the good obsidian supply they had in

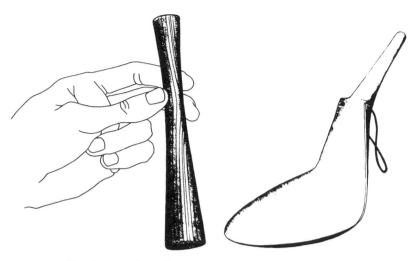

a. Pipe; b. Carved wooden spoon.

their territory, the Shasta were able to use these finely-made tools as a major trade item. The Shasta men made their blades and arrowheads by using a flaking technique—repeatedly striking the obsidian with a piece of deer antler to shape and sharpen it.

The men were responsible for almost all carving, which meant manufacturing the family's wooden spoons (sometimes instead made of bone or mussel shells), cooking paddles, and fire drills. The men also constructed wooden smoking pipes. These straight, trumpet-shaped pipes were made of a somewhat porous wood. The construction process involved soaking sticks of this wood in salmon oil, then inserting a salmon grub (taken from the family's store of dried salmon) into the deeply hollowed-out end of each stick. The pipemaker imprisoned the grubs in the sticks by blocking the entry holes, then hung the pipe sticks under the roof of the umma for the remainder of the winter. By spring, a few of the grubs would have bored their way through the pipe sticks to the other ends, leaving smooth and even smokeholes.

Men also spent a good bit of time making and repairing their fishing and hunting equipment and weapons. Iris cordage had to be made and woven for deer snares, and fishing nets had to be woven

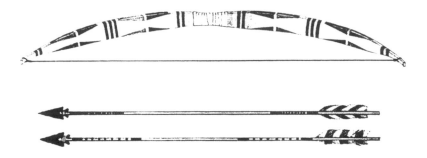

Bow and arrows.

from cordage the men wound from dogbane gathered along the rivers. Yew (or perhaps manzanita or syringa) bows had to be formed, smoothed, backed with sinew for strength, decorated with the hunter's personal painted design, and strung with sinew. Arrows had to be smoothed, straightened, and fitted out with hawk or perhaps grouse feathers that the men singed to give each a clean, straight line. Construction of hide arrow quivers, salmon spears, and perhaps woven stick and leather armor for raiding expeditions might also occupy the men and boys as they sat together in the wukwu during the winter days.

The women spent many cold winter days working in the umma, weaving tule mats and making the twined basketry used for cooking, storage, carrying, and even wearing (basket caps). Although some anthropologists have stated that the aboriginal Shasta did very little basketry work, and that in modern Shastan society the art has disappeared, contemporary Shasta dispute this and, in fact, cite several Shasta who today continue the traditional craft.

For their basket work, the women gathered hazel and willow rods for the upright (warp) foundation, and roots from the willow and pine for the base support frame. The actual twining itself was most often done with specially prepared yellow pine root, which the women had baked, steamed, then split into thin sheets. These materials could be stored after initial preparation, then taken out for use during a slack period in the gathering season (such as winter).

When the women actually began weaving the baskets, they reboiled and steamed the pine strips, split them into still finer lengths, and then dyed some of the strips with acorn shells for black and alder bark for red. Other decoration might be interwoven with basketgrass or maidenhair fern stems. Decorations such as the "salmon heart," the "flint goes around," and the "butterfly" designs usually had symbolic meanings. One expert on basketry, Gregory Schaaf, states that the Shasta baskets can be readily distinguished from other baskets of the region by the design appearing on the inside as well as the outside of the basket.

The baskets themselves were similar in sizes and shapes (as well as uses) to those constructed by other tribes of the area, particularly the Karuk, Yurok, and Hupa. The women made large and small storage baskets, generally wide-mouthed and not too deep; long, conical burden baskets; cooking baskets of varying sizes and depths; platter baskets that were wide-mouthed and shallow; small eating baskets (each individual had her or his own); fairly narrow-mouthed, smaller baskets for storing odds and ends; openwork

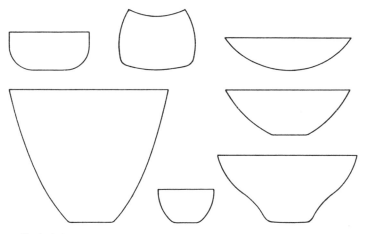

Basket shapes.

baskets for use as sieves; seed-beaters made from woven rawhide over a basketry frame; and open-weave cradleframe baskets for carrying infants.

Pregnancy and Childbirth

As the women and children rested and sorted acorns in the oak trees' shade, Tchuar-xia reached over and gently touched the tiny bow and arrow and the equally tiny apron that hung from her sister-in-law's belt.

It would be nice to have a new uma *[baby] in the family, Tchuar-xia thought, but she wished the child would come soon. She was tired of having to run ahead when she and her sister-in-law went out to gather wood or fetch water, searching to making sure no dead* huwatir *[rattlesnake] lay across the path and no* huquk *[grouse] were waiting in the bushes to surprise her sister-in-law into looking at them when she passed.*

Still, Tchuar-xia didn't want her new niece or nephew to be born blind or with the snake's scaly skin, nor with the wrinkled, red neck of the grouse. So the little girl always looked carefully along the paths and in the underbrush.

Tchuar-xia never forgot how, when she was small, she had seen with her own eyes the boy in her married sister's village who fell and thrashed around on the ground, making choking noises like a dying doe. When she had run in terror to her grandmother, the old woman had explained that the boy's mother had eaten the meat of a snared deer before her baby was born, and that a woman who was carrying a child, and even the child's father, had to guard their actions to keep the unborn child safe and healthy.

As soon as a couple knew they were expecting a child, their lives changed dramatically. Although taboos and traditions varied from tribe to tribe, throughout the Shastan culture the prospective parents were subject to rules governing activities and diet. Most regulations involved avoiding certain foods or actions that would transfer their qualities to the unborn child. Basketmaking, for example, might result in a child who was weak of arm and mind because the great concentration that weaving requires was thought to drain strength from the developing fetus. Similarly, a man could only hunt deer; killing a pheasant, for example, would result in a child afflicted with epilepsy. Eating rabbit meat might result in a child born with a hare-lip; eating anything deformed in any way might transfer that same disability to the child.

Toward the end of her pregnancy, the woman ate very little so that the coming child would not be so large that birthing would be difficult, and the man ceased hunting entirely. Both tied to their clothing a small fiber apron and a wooden bow and arrow. After the birth of the baby, during their individual postpartum periods of seclusion, the parents kept the apron if the child were female and the bow and arrow if the child were male.

The woman gave birth, assisted by an old woman relative, in the menstrual hut. If the labor was lengthy, the midwife or a shaman could prepare an herbal drink, sing, or tell sacred tales designed to ease delivery. One such story tells of how *Anakuna* ("large hawk") struggled to give birth to the five children he carried in his beak, but to no avail. Finally, he drank water from an eddy in the river, and immediately the children were all delivered safely. As this tale was told or sung, the laboring woman was given water from an eddy to drink.

As soon as the child was born, the umbilical cord was tied with a strand of the mother's hair and cut with an obsidian or stone knife. When the baby's remaining umbilicus fell off, it was wrapped and later ceremonially saved or disposed of by burial or burning. Until the cord fell off, the child was ritually bathed, massaged, and gently steamed in a basket over boiling water.

After the umbilicus had dropped off, the infant was wrapped in soft animal skins, which were often wadded with absorbent plant fibers, and placed in its first cradleframe. The child remained in this cradle during the mother's period of postpartum seclusion, which varied from tribe to tribe, ranging from five days to one month. During this period of seclusion, the new parents were again subject to strict dietary and activity taboos. A woman could scratch herself only with a specially carved scratching stick; she could not make baskets; she must eat sparingly and alone, abjuring meat; and she could not prepare her own food. The father was often required to leave the village, particularly during the first five days following the child's birth. He could eat only dried fish and acorns, and he could not hunt. Both the mother and the father took ritual sweats and baths during this time.

When the new mother's period of seclusion was over, she put her child into a new and larger cradle. In some groups, the old cradle was hung in a young and healthy tree outside the village, to ensure that the child would grow strong. The new cradle was laced from the bottom up if the baby was a boy and from the top down if a girl. The mother also attached small obsidian arrowheads or

knives to the cradle to ward off *Ta'matsi* ("small lizard"), who otherwise would come to tell the infant to be contrary in its behavior. Until it was old enough to crawl, the baby spent most of its time in the cradle, which often swung from the branch of a tree while the mother worked nearby.

Shasta infants were not given names until they reached one year of age. The actual process of name-giving varied from group to group; sometimes the parents chose the name, and at other times a relative had

Cradle basket. Courtesy of Fort Jones Museum.

this honor. Children were often named according to their own characteristics or hoped-for attributes, or a relative's attributes (in the hope that the child would show the same strengths). Thus a female child might be named *Kimpinuni* because she was a large baby, or *I'iawik* after a female relative who was known for her fancy beadwork. A male child might be given the name *Ahaiya*, after his father who, when he hunted deer, was so fast that he could run them down. Children might also be given the name of a relative who had been dead for more than one year. Among the Shasta Valley band a family member might give away or sell his or her name.

Childhood and Puberty

Gwatintin held his head high as he followed his father through the dusk to the wukwu. Tonight everyone would know that he, Gwatintin, youngest son of the house, was almost a man. He would have his own tule pillow mat set at his own place on the wukwu's floor, just like his older brothers, like his father, like the other men of the village.

His freshly pierced ears throbbed a little, but Gwatintin wasn't conscious of the pain. He thought with satisfaction of his cousins' upcoming visit from their village in the next valley. A smaller village than this, it had no wukwu, and when he had visited there, he had still been young enough to sleep inside the umma, and his older male cousins had just slept on the porch outside the umma. When they came to his village, though, Gwatintin would lead them with pride to proper sleeping quarters for men.

Later that night, as the men's talking and laughing died down, Gwatintin lay snuggled, warm and comfortable, in his deerskin robe. He was almost asleep when his father's uncle spoke, admonishing him not to wrap himself so tightly. "You're sleeping with the men now, su'gah [boy]," *the old man said sternly, "and we must be ready to wake up if an enemy comes." As the boy quickly tossed back the robe, his great uncle softened and added, "Good! Sleep*

*lightly covered, and after you swim in the cold river tomorrow
morning, you will earn yourself good luck!"*

Gwatintin smiled in the dark.

For Shasta children, as for children everywhere, childhood was
a mixture of play and instruction, during which they learned about
their society and about their own roles and responsibilities in that
society.

The old people in the village—especially grandparents and great
aunts and great uncles—were an important force in the children's
lives. As mentioned earlier, old people, especially women, were
the storytellers, retelling the sacred myths, such as the entertaining
and instructive tales of *Quatuk* ("coyote"), and the family's own
narrative tales and anecdotes. Through these sacred and secular
tales, the elders ensured that the tribe's children understood how
they and this land had been created especially for each other, and
how every Shasta had a responsibility to Mother Earth and all her
creatures. The tales taught how Quatuk had stolen fire from the
family of Pains and brought it to the people. He then laid down the
law that only men should carry fire drills, while the women should
carry the wood. And the children learned the story of Cricket and
how he mourned his dead child by covering himself with pitch,
teaching the Shasta to rub themselves black with ashes to mourn a
death.

The old people made sure the children knew the other stories
vital for their safety. They told of the lake- and river-dwelling
Xaseyauwat, the "sea dog," or of long-haired *Hika*, another water
monster that would grab an unwary swimmer and pull him down
to the bottom to his death. They warned the children against
playing in certain sacred spots in the mountains, for if the children
disturbed the peace of those spots, violent storms would arise.

Through the teachings of their elders, Shasta children knew that
a star close to the moon or a robin calling after dark was a bad
omen, that a whirlwind was really the dust of a dead shaman, that

thunder was the voice of the old man who lived in the east, and that the rainbow was painted by the sun shaman.

The old people (and other adults) also taught the children about the healing powers of certain plants. While serious illness was attended to by the village shaman or by the herbalist medicine woman or man, every Shasta knew how to gather *iknish* (wild celery root), which grew in dry, rocky areas in the valleys, to make tea for colds and headaches. The children learned that the white ashes of burned white oak bark placed on a cut or bruise would speed the healing, and that an elder could chew a piece of alder bark into a mash and spread it on a child's skin to sooth the itching of poison oak.

The elders directly instructed all the village children in appropriate behavior: "Never talk in the presence of your elders!" "Eat slowly, and not too much, so that people won't think you are ignorant and greedy!" A grandfather instructed his grandson specifically in the behavior of a man: "Work hard at your hunting because one day you will have a wife and children to feed. And," the old man might say, "if you want to be able to afford a fine bride, work hard to save and collect the woodpecker scalps and dentalium shells you will need." A grandmother would advise her granddaughter that it was becoming for a Shasta woman to be quiet and dignified, but not bashful or haughty. "When men visit from another village, Granddaughter, sit with your back to the fire, and neither talk nor laugh. Of course," she might add, "you may dance, and speak to any man who speaks first to you, but show that you respect yourself—a good man chooses a wife for her character."

Children were also instructed in their people's beliefs and lifeways through the use of the "prayer stick." Described by contemporary Shasta in *Survival and Adaptation Among the Shasta Indians*, the stick or staff was carved with symbols of such things as an eagle, a turtle, or a sunrise. Each of these symbols related to the tribe's creation myths, and the staff was used as a prompt in the storytelling process. As the story was told, the children sometimes acted it out.

During the day, very young children were generally kept with the women, taken along in cradleboards or packs if necessary, as the women went about their work. In that way, from an early age, the children learned by example to be industrious, and also felt a close part of the activity going on around them.

As the children grew older, boys generally spent most of their time with the men, and girls remained with the womenfolk. At this point, they began mimicking the activities of the adults, fashioning their own versions of tools, ornaments, tule mats, and so on. In this manner, the children began to learn the skills they would later practice as adults.

Childhood was marked by many rites of passage, some very formal and involved, some more casual, like the movement of the young boys from staying with the women to following the men. Childhood itself was clearly divided into stages of maturation. The importance the Shasta placed on this concept is evident by the different terms used for specific stages of maturity of both male and female children:

uma	baby, boy or girl
omaxia	boy or girl child just old enough to run around
qiaxa'hia	girl up to eight or nine years
wapaxo	girl from eight or nine to puberty
wapxe	pubescent girl
qiaxa	girl from puberty until marriage
wapso	girl/woman during menstruation
wapsahoa	bride until she first visits home
qiaxhapsi	20+ year-old unmarried woman
tari'chi	woman
su'kwahia	boy up to eight or nine years
su'kwa	boy from eight or nine to about fifteen years
gimpisu'kwa	boy from about fifteen until marriage

su'kwahapsi   20+ year-old unmarried man
awatikwa   man*

A boy's progress toward maturity was marked by several small-scale rites. When he reached the age of ten or twelve, each of his ears would be pierced with a porcupine quill. After this he would spend about five days on a vision quest alone in the hills, eating and sleeping little. When he returned, he would begin sleeping with the men in the wukwu, if the village had one, or on the porch area outside the door of his family's umma. A boy's first successful hunt was another maturation rite. It was marked by the ritual whipping of the boy by his father, who used his bowstring for this purpose.

A girl had her ears (and among some groups her nasal septum) pierced when she reached ten to twelve years of age, and at this time (or sometimes at puberty) an old woman in the village also tattooed her chin.

The Shastan tribes saved their most elaborate puberty rite—and, in fact, perhaps the most elaborate ritual of any they conducted—for a girl's first menses. The onset of menstruation meant a girl was coming into her powers, and very great powers they were as part of the female life force. Such a step had to be guided very carefully to protect the girl, the village, and the tribe.

The ceremony, beginning the evening of her first menses and lasting ten days, was attended by everyone in the village, as well as by members of villages far away, if the weather permitted. For the villagers and visitors, the ceremony was both a serious rite and a celebration, with days spent visiting with one another and nights spent singing and dancing.

For the girl, however, the rites of passage were rigorous. Secluded by day with her mother and/or an old woman (usually a

---

* These terms are taken from Catharine Holt, *Shasta Ethnology*, 343, and are based on information given her by Sargeant Sambo (Ah-Kee-Ah-Humpy), a Wiruwhitsu (Klamath River Valley Shasta).

relative) in the wapsahuumma (menstrual hut), save during ritual wood gathering expeditions, she was subject to strict taboos and duties. Her face was painted with red stripes, and her eyes were covered by a visor of blue jay feathers, sometimes completely, sometimes just enough so that she might not see the sun, moon, and stars, which could bring her ill fortune. Seated and always facing east, she could scratch herself only with the bone hisak (scratching stick), could eat little, and could speak only in a whisper to her attendant. During this time she shook a deer hoof rattle to keep herself awake. Most of each night was spent in dance, with the girl dancing alone or, as she tired, supported by two attendants, and again always facing east and away from the fire. She was allowed to sleep briefly just before dawn, but her attendant woke her frequently to ask if she had dreamed and to perform certain rituals to chase away evil portents brought on by certain dreams.

The dancing continued through each night and until noon on the last day, when the ceremony reached its climax. At noon, the girl's jay-feather visor was ceremonially removed, and she was taken away and bathed and dressed in her best. She then returned for a final dance, described by one source as a war dance. This same ritual (with some variations) was repeated, though in some groups for just five days, during the girl's next two menstrual periods, after which she was considered of marriageable age.

Shamans and Healing Rituals

Tchuar-xia shifted nervously from foot to foot and adjusted the straps of her burden basket. A little way ahead of her she could see her father and Gwatintin standing perfectly still. Around her, even the little children were quiet, and right in front of her, her new baby cousin, strapped into his cradleboard on his mother's back, silently blinked his wide eyes back at her.

The only sounds were the rustling of the breeze in the pine needles and, when the breeze died down, an old woman's voice rising and falling in song. Tchuar-xia tried to imagine what was

*going on ahead, up the trail and out of the travelers' sight. She
knew that the old woman shaman whose voice she could hear had
brought her medicine bundle along on this journey past the home
of the* achuha axaiki *[eagle spirit].*

*Before they had left the village, Tchuar-xia's mother had told her
that the path to her maternal grandmother's village led past one of
the places where a powerful* axaiki *[spirit] lived. Her mother had
said that the shaman would have to give the axaiki gifts of paint and
yellowhammer tail feathers, and would tell him that these people
were good people, whom he should let pass in peace.*

*But her mother hadn't told her what might happen if the eagle
axaiki wasn't satisfied with the gifts or if he didn't believe the
people were good. Tchuar-xia shivered, but stopped herself from
shifting the basket again. Nothing must distract the achuha axaiki
from listening to the shaman and accepting the gifts.*

Central to the Shastan people's religion was their belief in spirits
who inhabited trees, riversides, mountains, rocks, all the celestial
bodies, and many animals. They called the spirits *axaiki* (or *aheki*).
They were conceived as similar to humans in form (though much
smaller) and in personality, being helpful, contentious, greedy, and
capricious in turn. The axaiki lived in houses and quarreled
amongst themselves over who was most powerful, though they
never engaged in the humanlike competitions that, for example,
Greek and Roman gods did. These spirit people bear a strong
resemblance to the race of animal-humans that some of the sacred
Shasta myths describe as living on the earth before the Indian race
was created, though there is no clear link between them in the
Shasta legends. At any rate, the axaiki were not imaginary beings
to the Shasta. They were as real as other aspects of the world, from
rocks and trees to wind and fire, to coyotes and humans. The places
where they lived were avoided because of the axaikis' powers and
capricious natures. When a trail did run by a place inhabited by an
axaiki, a shaman or medicine woman performed a ceremony to
appease the spirit before the people passed by. If troubles later

occurred, the people assumed that the axaiki had not been pleased with the shaman's gifts.

All troubles might be attributed to the actions of the axaiki. Disease and death were caused by the axaiki shooting thin, icicle-like objects, called "pains" (also known as *axaiki*), into their victims' bodies. Bad luck could be caused by the presence of one of these axaiki-sent "pains" in one's home or village.

These same spirits were the source—in the form of patrons or guardians—of a shaman's power. A shaman, almost always a woman, had at least one axaiki she communicated with and received power from, though a shaman could always see all the axaiki and hear them singing around her. The personal axaiki were inherited, as a mother generally passed her shaman position to her daughter, or perhaps a niece. Occasionally a capricious axaiki might desert a family and transfer allegiance to another shaman, but apparently this was uncommon. A shaman was always very careful to please and placate her axaiki and to follow its instructions carefully.

In addition to her inherited axaiki, a shaman sometimes tried to attract the patronage of the unassigned, independent spirits, some of whom might even be more powerful than her original axaiki. The grizzly bear axaiki was the most desirable and the most powerful axaiki, because the grizzly was related to the Shasta, according to their creation legend. The shaman who could call upon the grizzly axaiki, and some accounts say that this shaman had to be a male, was the most powerful of the Shasta shamans. The rattlesnake axaiki was also very powerful. Its medicine could cure—and even prevent—a rattlesnake bite, as well as provide other powers to its shaman.

The power and importance of a village shaman was great. She looked after the health of her village in all respects, from rituals to assure good luck in childbirth and gambling, to ceremonies to ward off evil, to actual physical doctoring. Her position, however, was not an enviable one. With her great power came grave responsibilities, and she could be put to death for not fulfilling any of her many duties.

A shaman might not, in fact, be a particularly popular figure in the village, though her pronouncements were respected and followed. The shaman was also strictly bound by social and behavioral restrictions. For example, she could not take part in general or recreational dancing (excluding the puberty dance, which was both ritual and recreational). She could not play gambling games, since she had the unfair advantage of being able to control everyone's luck. She could not attend funerals other than those for her family members residing in the village, and even then she could not shed tears because that would bring sickness and trouble upon the village. The actions—and even the emotions—of a shaman were severely restricted.

So why would any female choose such an uncomfortable role? Actually, choice was rarely involved. An apprentice shaman was chosen by her mother (or perhaps aunt) in childhood and thereafter spent most of her time with the shaman. For the child, perhaps, the initial singling out was exciting, setting her clearly above her playmates in importance to the whole village. She was painted when the shaman painted herself, and the shaman would give her instruction in behavior and rites.

During this period, the child would watch, mimic, and learn, waiting for a sign—sent by the axaiki—that she was meant to be a shaman. Later, the sign would come; shamans were rarely mistaken in their choices of novices. The girl's vocation would be confirmed to her by recurring cycles of dreams or nightmares, often featuring swarms of yellow jackets, which were thought to represent the axaiki. At this point, whether she had tired of the training and restrictions or not, whether she wished to become her village's shaman or not, the girl was committed to her destiny. To deny her vocation when dreams had manifested it could bring sickness and even death to herself, to members of her family, and to people in her village.

Although a novice shaman inherited her mother's or aunt's position and axaiki, at the onset of the dream period she had to begin collecting her own accoutrements. This was an exhaustive list, and included buckskins, wolfskins, silvergray fox skins, coyote skins, otter skins, fisher skins, small dish baskets, small bowl baskets, tail and wing feathers of the eagle, and the tails of yellowhammers and large woodpeckers. The girl was required to collect all of the items in increments of ten each (the Shastan tribes' sacred numbers were five and ten), so that gathering her complete paraphernalia could take a prospective shaman many years. This too, of course, was part of the plan and ritual. As she gathered her skins and feathers, the girl came to know the mountains, the valleys, and the creatures and plants living there. She learned to feel the powers of the many axaiki dwelling throughout the land. As she made her baskets, the girl prayed and meditated to strengthen her spiritual side. All this readied her for actual contact with her own powerful axaiki.

In addition to the shamanic items needed in groups of ten, the girl had to collect specific doctoring tools, such as a buckskin pierced with holes; red, yellow, and blue paints; and a pipe. The requirements for her personal ornamentation varied, depending upon her axaiki.

During this period of gathering tools and preparing herself, the novice continued to have dreams manifested by the axaiki. After she had had several of the portentous dreams, a dream would come in which she would hear a voice speaking above her head. When she turned to look, her axaiki would be revealed to her, standing behind her and pointing a drawn bow and arrow at her heart. At this stage, the novice would sink deeper into sleep, into a trance, and would lie rigid until sunset. During the trance, her axaiki would appear again to her and, showing it accepted her, would sing her its song (each axaiki had its own song), telling her its name and where it dwelt. In the evening, as she began to revive, the novice would murmur, over and over again, the song and the axaiki's name. Eventually she would rise and begin to dance.

For five nights (again, the sacred number) the girl continued this dancing in the okwaumma or before an open fire in the center of the village. During the daylight hours she slept, occasionally waking to sip acorn gruel. On the third, fourth, and fifth nights of her dance, her axaiki would appear to her and shoot the icicle-like "pains" into her, so that she would have her shaman powers. At times she would react with a sort of seizure. When she revived, she would perform disappearance and reappearance feats with the "pains" in various parts of her body, demonstrating her control of them. All shamans had at least three "pains" permanently housed in their bodies—one in each shoulder and one in the back of the head—which gave them their powers. In addition, during her initiation dance, the novice had two "pains" in her heels which enabled her to dance the requisite five nights.

The apprentice shaman followed the dance ceremony with a ten-day fast, after which she went back to her customary activities, though in a subdued fashion. Now her family helped gather what remaining animal skins and other items she required. If everything was gathered by the following winter, the novice would then have her "qualifying dance," this one of three nights' duration. The final step in the long process of becoming a shaman was one of the major celebration ceremonies of the Shasta, and all the girl's friends and relatives came, as did all neighboring villagers.

In this ceremony, while her male helper called to the novice shaman's axaiki, the young woman danced to draw her axaiki to a pole her father had painted, befeathered, and erected in the axaiki's honor. The would-be shaman's relatives would then tie each item of her equipment to the pole to prove her readiness when the axaiki called out for it. At midnight each night, the axaiki appeared, and while it took its time looking around the village, the novice slept for a few hours. At the same time, her helper smoked, and the villagers and guests ate and smoked quietly. In the powerful presence of the axaiki (seen only by the novice), all conversation was very subdued. Before daybreak each night, the axaiki had to be danced back to its home again, pausing on its journey each time the girl paused in her dance. This sequence was repeated until, after the third night, the novice became recognized as a fully qualified shaman. Still, the young woman was obligated to repeat the dance sequence for five winters—sometimes even for ten winters—to build up her powers and strengthen her relationship with her axaiki.

Even after going through this rigorous training, however, a woman might not be allowed to practice if her mentor was still alive and active herself. When her mentor shaman died, the new shaman could then take up her calling, but only after she took the dead shaman's paraphernalia to the forest and hung it from the branches of a tree to be naturally destroyed by the elements.

An active shaman's duties to her village were many. She was, of course, a doctor. Since almost all major injuries and illnesses were believed to be caused by axaiki "pains," her doctoring ritual called for removing the "pains" from the patient's body. This ritual, too, was fairly elaborate because of the dangers involved in handling any of the icicle-like objects. A typical cure began with elaborate preparations. The shaman first set up a covered basket of water, then dispersed drops of paint into the air or into the fireplace to put the axaiki into good humor. Friends and neighbors began singing (again, to please the axaiki), and the shaman smoked, generally outside the village. During this time her axaiki told her about the case.

Once the actual cure got underway, the shaman sang and danced as her axaiki had instructed, occasionally seizing small, broken pieces of "pains" from the patient's body as she went. The small pieces sometimes represented miscellaneous aches or pains. Other small pieces might be "red herrings" put there by the axaiki that was causing the illness in the hope of deceiving the shaman. After a time, the shaman would suck a red, black, or yellow clotted substance from the site of the pain, which then cleared the way for the dramatic capture of the actual illness-causing "pain." In the middle of her dancing and singing, the shaman would suddenly break off, rush to the patient, grab the "pain," and quickly thrust it into the waiting basket of water.

The cure was not yet completed, however. The shaman had then to dispose of the "pain" by throwing it in the direction of the axaiki who had sent it, or by placing it, along with various herbs, in a mussel shell and burying it in the fire's embers. If, however, the "pain" had been sent by another shaman (often at the request of an enemy of the victim), it would be broken, immediately causing the sender's death. The shaman concluded her curing procedure by again sucking at the site of the now-removed "pain."

A shaman could never refuse her duty of caring for the people of her village. If, however, she could not effect a cure, or if she felt the axaiki causing the illness was stronger than her own axaiki, she could suggest calling in another shaman who had a more powerful axaiki or who had an axaiki with specialized powers. If she attempted a cure but was unsuccessful, she had to return half or all of her fee.

A shaman had additional duties connected with the "pains." Sometimes a household, or even an entire village, might suspect that a "pain" had been placed in its vicinity by enemies, causing ill luck, sickness, or death. In this case, a shaman would be called in to remove it. This belief explains much of the Shasta's fear and feeling of helplessness when the whites came and brought with them epidemics of smallpox, measles, and other diseases, against which the shamans had no power. As one informant explained, the axaiki (and thus the shamans, too) had no powers against the whites "because white people have a different scent and the axaiki can't stand it" (Sargeant Sambo quoted in Holt 1946, 331).

In other situations, a shaman might be hired to curse enemies, rejected (or rejecting) lovers, or rivals, smiting them with "pains." A shaman might be called upon to locate lost or stolen property or even people, as well as the culprits responsible. A shaman was also responsible for propitiating, through songs, dances, and gifts, axaiki in the territory through which hunters had to travel and those in areas where food must be gathered.

Similar to the shamans, but not holding the same great powers, were medicine people. These people, who might be men or women, knew how to make "medicine bundles" of secret and powerful objects that would bring their purchasers luck, for example in gambling, hunting, or fishing. The medicine men and women could produce love powders from plants, or they might be requested to produce rain through a specialized ceremony. The power to be a medicine man or woman ran in certain families, though, as with shamans, only one family member could practice at any one time.

Medicine people could also heal. Miss Clara Wicks, a Scott Valley Shasta, describes the healing practices and practitioners when she was a little girl, before the turn of the century:

Grandma used to be a sort of doctor. They used to call on her every time somebody had a little ailment. She would go over there and she would dress up with her feathers made out of yellowhammer and blue jays and other feathers. She had bracelets, and I think she had some on her head and on her neck. A big bunch of feathers hung down her shoulders. And she used to sing and dance and sprinkle this liquid over with fir boughs. Sometimes the doctor[s] would put their hands on and press where they got pain, and their patients would get well.

One time I used to have an awful headache. I almost died with headache day after day. I just had to go to bed and couldn't raise my head up. One day my mother's aunt came down. She had been up at Tyee Jim's place—he lived about a mile from our place. She said, "Can you make it up to Tyee Jim's? Old Henry Jo came out, and I want to see if he can doctor you and do something for that headache you got. Maybe he can help." And I said, "Well, maybe I can make it up there." So I just barely made it, I was so weak and sick.

They made a bed for me. They put a comfort and pillow on the floor, and they told me to lay down there. He had stripped his shirt off and rolled his pants up above his knees and he was barefooted, and a bunch of fir boughs in his hands and a bowl of liquid sitting on the floor. I lay down and he started to sing and dance up and down—tip his heel and toe up, and all the others started singing and he dipped that fir into the liquid and sprinkled that over me. They kept singing and he dipped the boughs in the liquid and rubbed it across my forehead twice, and he got through singing. "Now," he said, "I think you will be all right." So I kind of wiped my face off a little bit. I got up and went home that evening.

I was pretty tired but I didn't have a headache. I went to bed with no headache.

Next morning I got up. I feel like I was in a different world. Everything seemed so clear. I just felt so nice and you know, I never had a headache since. Lots of times I would be so sick I was just about ready to die, but I never had a headache. I never did have headaches since that day. I could smell the celery root in that water—I could smell that celery root. [*]

Death and Burial

The grandmother's voice rose and fell in the smoky darkness. "Quatuk [coyote] looked at the people crying around him. 'What shall we do? What shall we do?' they kept crying to him. And Cricket cried the loudest of all. 'My child, my child! We must bring him back to life!' But Quatuk shook his head." The old woman paused and looked around at the circle of young faces.

Outside, the winter wind whistled around the corners of the umma. Tchuar-xia shivered, though the fire burned in its stone hearth behind her. She'd heard this story of how death came to the

* From Pat Martin, "Stories by Clara Wicks" in the 1971 *Siskiyou Pioneer and Yearbook*, pp. 60-61. Reprinted courtesy of the Siskiyou County Historical Society.

people many times, but each time, at the point when Quatuk carelessly shook his head, she felt the brush of what-might-have-been *across the back of her neck.*

The flames sent shadows shifting across the grandmother's face as she continued. "'No,' said Quatuk, 'the world would be too crowded, and we would begin falling off into the encircling ocean. The dead must stay dead.' So the people mourned, they buried Cricket's child, and they sweated for five days, but they wished Quatuk's child would also die.

"And Quatuk's child did die, and then Quatuk cried that the dead should come back to life after all. 'But, Quatuk,' answered all the people, 'you said when Cricket's child died that the world would be too full if no one died.'

"'I've changed my mind,' cried Quatuk. 'Let Cricket's child also come back!'

"'No,' said Cricket, who was still mourning, and who had completely covered himself with pitch to show his mourning. 'My child cannot be brought back. He has decayed. As you said, the dead must remain dead.'"

Again the old woman paused, and she looked at each of the children in turn. "And so Quatuk buried his child and sweated and mourned, and rubbed himself with pitch. And that is how death first came to the people, and that is why the dead can never be brought back to life."

The Shasta treated death with the elaborate ritual given all the great mysteries. Prescribed procedures governed the treatment of the body, burial, the mourning process for survivors, and the cleansing of the funeral participants. While some points differed among the different Shastan tribes, most followed the same pattern.

When a Shasta died indoors, his or her family removed the body through an opening made in the building's roof or wall. Bringing the body through the door of the house would bring bad luck to the household. The opening was always cut in the east side of the house because the dead person's soul traveled east toward daylight (sunrise). After the body's removal, the survivors purified the house, burning aromatic roots such as *qarawihu'* (Helianthus cusickii) to chase away any lingering axaiki.

Before the body was removed for burial, female relatives washed it in cold water with wormwood leaves, and dressed it. The women put the best clothes on the corpse, along with bead necklaces, dentalium ornaments, and other valuables. When the body had been fully prepared, it was lain in state outside the house. At this point, relatives and friends gathered to dance and lament around the body. Waving fir branches, they called out to the dead, reminding him that he was going to another world and asking him to take all their troubles away with him. All the mourners, some of whom might have come from a great distance, laid strings of dentalium currency or other valuables across the body. The mourners danced and lamented in shifts, one group taking the place of another as the dancers tired, for as long as four or five days to ensure that all relatives had a chance to arrive for the ceremony.

When relatives or friends had dug the grave and all the mourners had gathered, three or four pallbearers carried the body to the gravesite. The mourners followed, still dancing, wailing, and carrying the fir branches with which they would line the grave. Before the body was interred, the headman spoke to those assembled and then redistributed some of the funerary gifts and the property of the deceased to the mourners. When the body, wrapped in animal skins, was laid in the grave, it was placed on its back with the head to the east. The mourners then filled in the grave, placing a layer of sand on the top, and erected a fence of short fir poles around the grave. Baskets were sometimes placed atop the poles.

After the burial was completed, all the mourners bathed in a nearby river or stream before returning to the village. Those not directly involved with the preparation of the corpse or the gravedigging then left. The others swept and thoroughly cleaned the deceased's umma, then burned the sweepings, as well as many of the belongings of the deceased. Occasionally the umma itself was burned, and if the deceased had been the village headman, and thus the owner of the okwaumma, both his house and the meeting house might be burned.

For the near relatives and those contaminated by contact with the corpse or the grave, the burial and cleanup were followed by a five-day fast and ritual sweat for purification. Parents who had lost a child, and widows or widowers, cut or burned their hair short, and made a mourning belt from the hair. The women also rubbed their faces and sometimes their heads with pitch and charcoal. The widows and widowers maintained the short hair and face blackening until remarriage. Additional fasting (especially avoidance of meats) lasting up to one month, plus other taboos and purification rites, were required of widows and the parents of a stillborn child. All members of the community avoided speaking the name of the deceased, sometimes indefinitely, sometimes until the name had been regiven to an infant.

While some Shastan groups had formal cemeteries outside the villages, family grave plots were equally common, with a wife being buried in her husband's family plot. Being buried in one's homeland was very important to a Shasta. If a person died far from home, he or she might be cremated there, but then the relatives could carry the ashes home for burial.

Existent pre-contact accounts and myths do not elaborate on a concept of afterlife, but the Shasta had a strong belief, one that continues today, in the possibility of communion with the spirits of the dead.

Burial sites held (and still hold) tremendous importance as sacred places and as "the tangible evidence of a network of past kin ties" (Winthrop 1986, 60). Present-day Shasta have described how children were traditionally taught about where family members were buried, as well as where in the complex web of interrelationships each deceased person fit. Men and women might visit a family grave site as a reminder and reaffirmation of who they were in relation to their ancestors and as a place to be in communication with a deceased relative who might be able to give them comfort or advice.

Chapter 3

Mythology

For the traditional Shasta, their religion was and continues to be inseparable from their way of life. Shasta beliefs are grounded in *holism*, that is, in an understanding that all aspects of life are part of religion and ritual, and thus religious ritual is an integral part of all activities. Further, the holistic view of life ascribes mystic power as well as life force to everything—to all creatures, elements, and physical components of the world. The natural and the supernatural are joined together in Shastan reality.

Shasta mythology reflects these beliefs in both obvious and subtle ways. The majority of the collected myths deal with "animal-people" and "element-people": Coyote, Eagle, Raven, Wind, Thunder, and so on. The mythology of some Native American tribes describes an actual prehuman time when the animals walked, talked, and carried on their daily lives with one another. Shasta mythology makes no such distinction; myths about animals interacting with one another, as well as myths about animals and humans interacting, are most often presented as though they took place just yesterday.

This leads to another important aspect of Shasta, and most Native American, mythology: Myths are not just cute or clever stories to explain natural phenomena, to entertain children and adults, and to teach cultural mores. Myths do perform these functions, for American Indians have a lively appreciation of the ridiculous, an earthy sense of humor (especially visible in some of the bawdy Coyote stories), and a firm belief in the importance of teaching the children and all members of the tribe the traditional ways. But myths are also, as Kiowa writer N. Scott Momaday has said, "truth—a higher truth." And as such, they are timeless and sacred.

The published collections of Shasta myths contain slightly varying versions of many of the tribes' myths. Some sources also present conflicting myths on such subjects as the peopling of the earth. The myth with which this book opens, for example, is just one version of how the Shastan tribes came into being. Another version tells of Eagle sending down his two children, a boy and a girl, who became the progenitors of the Shastan people. Another source says that Waka, the Great Spirit, created the Shastan people himself, placing them on the spot he had specially chosen for them on Mother Earth.

Many Shasta myths feature Quatuk, "Coyote," the Shastan people's trickster-hero figure. He is similar to the Coyote of the southwestern and plains tribes' myths, to the Raven of some of the northwest coast groups, and to the Rabbit in the tales of the Algonquians. Coyote is lusty, wily, greedy, cowardly, and sometimes foolish; he is also just as often smarter than all the other people, and he often uses his cleverness to help his fellows.

Shasta myths share themes and plots with the mythologies of neighboring tribes. They have in common such themes as the grievous results of incest, the temptation motif, the humble succeeding when the stronger could not; and such plots as bringing a loved one back from the dead, or testing a son-in-law or prospective son-in-law. They also share basic elements with the mythologies of all peoples, for example, flood stories and geospecific references in myths.

The following three myths are representative and do not appear in popular anthologies. These myths are fairly short. Many Shasta myths, however, such as "The Magic Ball" and "The Lost Brother," are much longer, multi-episode stories, with subplots and multiple morals and how-and-why explanations within them.

Why the Animals Are Hot-Blooded

(Based on a version published by L. M. Burns in *Land of Sunshine*.)

When the earth was in its first days, the animals were cold. On the whole earth there was only one large hot rock for them to warm themselves by. Lynx owned this rock, but the jealousy of all the animals was so great that Lynx agreed to hold a gambling game to determine who would keep the rock. So Lynx called all the animals except Quatuk to come to the Klamath to try their luck.

Quatuk, sitting alone twenty miles away in Shasta Valley, heard them playing. "Oh," he said to himself, "I will play them a trick." First he draped an animal skin over his head and shoulders, and then Quatuk ran over the hills to the gambling game. As he ran, he sang his traveling song: "Tach-a-nee! Tach-a-nee! Tach-a-nee!"

When Quatuk came up to the gambling game, he saw that Lynx still had the rock. So Quatuk, completely covered by the animal skin, joined the game. He was a clever and lucky gambler, and soon he had won. But still, the rock was so hot that only Lynx could touch it, and Quatuk was sure that Lynx planned to play him a trick to keep the rock.

When all the animals began to dance, Quatuk joined in. Covered by the skin, he leapt higher than anyone. But as he danced he watched Lynx, and he saw that Lynx was plotting to kill him. Still leaping high, Quatuk suddenly slipped from under the skin cloak, leaving it to continue dancing for him, and hid in the shadows.

Suddenly, as the dance grew wilder and wilder, Lynx seized the rock and threw it with all his might at Quatuk's dancing cloak. The animal skin cloak only fell gently to the ground as the rock brushed it. But the hot rock itself continued flying through the air until it hit the side of the mountain, where it broke into a hundred pieces.

The drake immediately stopped dancing and ran to grab a piece of the stone. Tucking a fragment under his arm, he ran away—and you know that he still carries it there to this day, for isn't the drake warmer under his left wing than under his right?

After the drake had grabbed his piece and run away, all the other dancing animals, and Quatuk too, broke from the circle and ran to seize pieces of warmth for themselves. But some were too late. Those that were too slow to get even the smallest pinch of the rock crawled away to the water or into the earth. There they hid, cold and sluggish, from the scorn of the others. And so they remain to this day.

Why Frogs are in the Water

(Based on a version published by Edward S. Curtis in *The North American Indian*.)

One day one of the people asked Frog, "Do you bathe your children? Do you take them to swim?"

"No," Frog answered.

"You ought to, you know," said the one.

So Frog took up one of his children and threw him into the river.

"Where is your child?" Frog was asked.

He answered, "I threw him into the river."

"But," the other said, "that is not what I told you to do. I said you should bathe your child."

"Well, he is in the river now," Frog answered. "Let him stay there."

Blue Jay

(Based on a version collected by Catharine Holt in her unpublished manuscript *Shasta Myths*, in the Bancroft Library, University of California, Berkeley.)

One day Blue Jay was out hunting elk, and chased one down near a village, near Seiad, where he killed it. Blue Jay looked so pretty and fine that some girls decided he was the prettiest young man any of them had ever seen, so they let him come and live with them.

All the women of the village (and there are no men mentioned, so maybe it was just a village of women) at first thought Blue Jay was fine, so they allowed him to stay. But all he did was stand or sit around, and so the women got to talking. "He doesn't take a bath. He doesn't do anything. What's the matter with him?" they said among themselves. But still they let him stay because he was so pretty, especially his legs, which were just perfect.

One day some of the girls decided to play a trick. They went to a place up the river, got hold of a rotten log, and fixed some deer horns on it. Then they sent the log floating down the river. All the women in the village saw the horns in the river and talked and then screamed about the deer out there, and how somebody should go out and kill it. But Blue Jay had no bow and arrows. He couldn't swim. He couldn't do anything.

So the women got angry, and they rushed up to Blue Jay and began to tear off his clothes so that he could swim out to the deer. But when they pulled off his leggings, sand came pouring out from where he had packed it in to give his legs such fine form, and he was left standing there with those skinny legs like he has now.

Well, Blue Jay was kicked out of the village. But before he left, he stole a bag full of acorns that the old women had gathered. He stole away up this way, and when the village people began to chase him, he rose up into the sky so they couldn't reach him. But he began to get tired, and as he was coming over the ridge near Horse Creek here, he dropped his sack, and the acorns scattered all around. And that is why, though only down-the-river people had them before, we have so many acorns here, more than anywhere else.

Chapter 4

An Enduring People:
The Shastan Tribes, 1820s to Present

"It was not good to be a California Indian in the 1850s," wrote historian William Brandon (1961, 305). A staggering number of statistics support his statement. The California Indians, he continues, "were killed off in what seems to have been the biggest single spree of massacring in American history. Some guesses say 30,000 [of more than 300,000] were left by 1859. These had dwindled to roughly 15,000 by the end of the century." Yet how many think of the California Indians when they consider the ravages made upon the native populations of North America in the past few centuries?

The history of the American Indian peoples is—across the entire continent—a story of exploitation, deception, and outright extermination. That the holocaust was of greatest proportions in California can be explained by two basic facts.

First, the frontier process in California was highly accelerated compared to the settling of the East and Midwest. Although ranchos were established prior to the mid-nineteenth century, the initial large-scale invasion of the Northwest was fueled not by a desire to find peace, freedom, or even just a place to make a new home (as was the case in the rest of the country to some extent) but rather by greed for gold. The hordes pouring into California during the gold rush decade of 1848-1858 sought simply to take as much as possible as quickly as possible by whatever methods necessary. The Indians were generally viewed as either a ready labor force or as a relatively unimportant but bothersome impediment to these miners. Even as the accelerated settlement of California took place, with ranches and small towns supplanting mining claims and camps, the attitude was mostly the same. While their usefulness as workers was acknowledged, their resistance to "progress" most often met with a harsh response. "Let our motto be extermination, and death to all opposers," proclaimed a newspaper in the gold rush town of Yreka (quoted in Brandon 1961, 311).

The second major difference between the situation in California and that of the rest of the continent was that the Californian Indians were among the most gentle and "primitive" of North America's aboriginal peoples. Most were simply not warlike. Warfare among California Indians was usually carried on only in retaliation for a wrong. They were generally at peace and in harmony with their environment, and that very harmony—exemplified in their view of nature and themselves as parts of a whole and their acceptance of what life offered them—branded the California Indians as hopelessly ignorant, lazy, backward, and ignoble in the eyes of many of the whites.

California Indians thus received less of the respect and admiration from their conquerors that the more warlike and defiant Eastern and Plains Indians did. Ranchers who hired them did respect their intelligence and hard work. Powers mentions that they were given more demanding and complicated tasks, and higher pay as well (1877, 401). Still, the California Indians were frequently seen, as a government inspector matter-of-factly wrote in 1858, as sacrifices for the "great cause of civilization which, in the nature and course of things, must exterminate the Indians" (quoted in Brandon 1961, 305).

First White Contacts

The first recorded contacts the Indians of the Klamath, Scott, and Shasta river valleys had with whites were with fur traders in the 1820s and 1830s. Explorers, most often with the Hudson's Bay Company, came through the valleys trapping and collecting pelts. Scott Valley, a particularly rich area, was known to the trappers as "Beaver Valley," and in one month in the winter of 1836, trapper Thomas McKay collected 1,800 beaver pelts. Many of the pelts were obtained through trade with the Shasta, who took glass beads, small mirrors, and axes in return for the skins. The Shasta used the beads and mirrors in weaving and basketry, and on clothing, necklaces, and belts.

The generally peaceable trappers and the early settlers also brought, however, European diseases, such as measles, malaria, and smallpox, all of which had devastating effects on the defenseless Indian population. One Shasta account tells of the death by smallpox of an entire village at Humbug Creek.

Mid-1800s: The Goldrush and Its Aftermath

The wholesale disruption of the Shastan tribes' lifeways and habitat was completed with the discovery of gold, first along the Trinity and Klamath rivers in 1850, and then at Scott Bar and Thompson's Dry Diggings in 1851–1852. The 1850s saw the influx of miners and ranchers, the large scale settlement of Yreka and other small towns throughout Shasta territories, and the establishment in 1852 of a permanent military presence at Fort Jones in Scott Valley to protect the white miners and settlers. By 1853, Yreka itself had an estimated population of 10,000.

The miners and the ranchers wanted, of course, the same lands that the Shastan tribes had already settled along the rivers and streams and in the fertile valleys. As the Shasta were driven away from their villages and their fishing and hunting grounds, they lost their means of support. By the 1850s, government reporters were already writing of the "great state of destitution" of the Shasta, and of the often wanton murdering of the native peoples (Gibbs [1853] 1972, 59). Treaties were signed and broken, and reservation lands or "reserves" were arranged and rearranged during this period. As George Gibbs ([1853] 1972, 72-73) wrote in his journal of Colonel Redick McKee's 1851 expedition into northwestern California, the treaties were designed to "embrace, in as compact a space as possible," lands for the native population, while "leav[ing] the most valuable mineral lands" as well as tillable farming and ranching lands to the whites.

Nonetheless, the Shasta did agree to and sign treaties during this time, though the United States Senate later refused to ratify them. One of these treaties, the treaty of November 1851 that Gibbs writes of, holds particular infamy in Shasta history. According to accounts by several Shasta informants, the treaty, signed near Quartz Valley by thirteen Shastan tribal chiefs, was to be celebrated by a feast prepared by the soldiers to which all the Shastan tribes were invited. Some accounts state that three thousand warriors, most of the Shasta adult male population, came to the feast, at which they were served beef laced with strychnine. All but 150 of those invited died, some there at the white's camp and some along the trails home. Survivors' accounts tell of spending weeks collecting and burying bodies found along the trails back to the villages.

As might be expected, official government documents in regard to this poisoning are difficult to come by, though there are newspaper and government reports of other poisonings of Indian populations. Gibbs (1972) himself mentions in his entry for October 28, 1851 (seven days before the treaty signing) that "We learned from every quarter, that apprehensions existed that the object of assembling them was to kill the whole together." His entry regarding the signing of the treaty, however, merely states that "In the afternoon it was signed in the presence of a large concourse of whites and Indians....The usual presents were then distributed, and they separated in very good humor." Later local newspaper stories, however, matter-of-factly refer to "the poisoning of 1851" as a historical fact.

A good many incidents and outbreaks of violence characterized Shasta-white relations during the 1850s. Roving bands of white vigilantes and bands of Shastas out to revenge wrongs they experienced were in frequent conflict. California Shasta bands also joined with the Rogue River Shasta, the Klamath, the Takelma, and the Tututni in the Rogue River Wars, which reached their height in 1855-1856. One result of this particular war, which the Indians lost to the superior white forces, was that the Rogue River Shasta, as well as some members of California Shasta tribes, were placed on the Grande Ronde and Siletz reservations on Oregon's coast, far from their ancestral lands and their traditional lifestyle.

Some Shasta families in northern California did find refuge with supportive white ranchers, such as the Burtons in Scott Valley. Many Shasta women who had married white miners and ranchers, however, were still ordered to leave, taking their children with them, to join forced marches to the disease-plagued reservations in the Sacramento Valley.

The Shasta and other Indian groups were also subject to widespread kidnapings; women and young girls were taken for concubinage, and Indians of both sexes were taken for forced labor. Indian slavery was, in fact, institutionalized by the California legislature in 1850 when it adopted a law allowing any Indian to be declared "vagabond" and thereafter sold as a laborer to the highest bidder. "Vagrancy" and "vagabonding" became common as Indians were pushed off their homelands and away from their sources of sustenance. As historian Jack Forbes (1969, 61) writes: "The fact that the whites of California and the Great Basin desired cheap labor was certainly a major factor in preventing the establishment of adequate reservations."

Molly Oscar and her grandchildren. Courtesy of Siskiyou County Historical Society.

Red Bird. Courtesy of Siskiyou County Historical Society.

Sargeant Sambo, Ah-Kee-Ah-Humpy. Courtesy of Siskiyou County Historical Society.

"We Shall Live Again":
The 1870s Ghost Dance Movements

Through the Ghost Dance movements of the 1870s, the participating tribes sought to "assure survival by increasing their numbers through returning the dead to life" (Thornton 1986, xi). The movements, particularly the earlier phases, focused on the return of the dead and of the earlier times when the Indians held control of their lands, when game was plentiful, and when traditional lifeways were practiced. The living Indians' own part in this dramatic change involved performing round dances and singing. All versions, and particularly the later Earth Lodge Cult and the Big Head Cult, emphasized sacred dreams, in which the dreamer's dead relatives and tribesmen appeared and gave her or him spiritually powerful songs and advice.

The Shasta were much involved in three waves of the Ghost Dance religion. The first movement, which reached them in 1871 from the Tule Lake Modoc, they in turn spread to the Karuk and to their relatives and the other Indians on the Siletz and Grand Ronde reservations. The second wave, the Earth Lodge Cult, was spread to the Shasta from the McCloud Wintu in 1871-1872; Shastas then spread the cult northward to the Siletz and Grande Ronde reservations, where it became known as the Warm House Dance. The third wave, occurring in the mid-1870s, involved the Shasta in an offshoot of the concurrently practiced Pomo and Patwin Bole-Maru movement, called the Big Head Cult. This movement, which involved elaborate feather headdresses and other regalia, again came from the south to the Shasta, who carried it northward.

The Ghost Dance movement involved ritual dances, lasting several days, often held in specially constructed long houses. During the dancing and singing, participants experienced trances in which the dead appeared and offered advice and instructions in healing, behavior, and, as one informant related, instruction in "how to be happy" (Sargeant Sambo quoted in Dubois 1946, 14).

Got-a-uke Ek su [Daylight—looking for it]. Called "Rising Sun." Courtesy of Siskiyou County Historical Society.

This visionary revivalist movement offered the destitute Indians hope in the face of the patently hopeless onslought of white incursion and control.

Government Relations and Cultural Survival, 1880s to Present

By the 1880s, with the quelling of the Modoc resistance led by Kintpuash (also called Captain Jack) in 1873, white settlers and the combined force of the United States and California governments had taken control of northern California. For the next one hundred years, then, the Shastas' fight to maintain their culture and unity took on a different form, as the battle tactics of the whites moved from physical genocide to forced assimilation of the native peoples as individuals rather than as tribal peoples. This was carried out, among other ways, by land allotment policies, giving small tracts of land to individuals rather than to whole tribes.

Because no ratified treaty existed, the Shastas received only limited allotments of lands, though those they did receive (for example, on Meamber Gulch, on Moffett Creek near Fort Jones, on Bogus Creek, and at Walker Bar near Hamburg) became gathering places and even refuges for large groups of homeless and destitute Shastas.

The people began to fight through the legal system for their rights, working with such statewide organizations as the Indian Board of Co-operation in the 1920s and the Indian Claims Commission beginning in the 1940s (and continuing through the 1970s) to secure reparations for lands taken from them. This latter work resulted in payments of $600 per person in 1973. The 1934 Indian Reorganization Act also gave organizing Shastas the opportunity to form the Quartz Valley Rancheria, first built upon and occupied in 1940. The rancheria was later terminated (in 1958), as were several others in the state, as a result of new government policies. The rancheria was reinstated in the early 1980s, again as a result of work through the legal system by California Indians. Since 1980,

Shastas have been working to achieve federal recognition for their nation and to protect such physical aspects of their heritage as burial sites threatened by development.

The survival of the Shasta culture has depended on more than legal battles for land, however. The United States Forest Service report, produced jointly by the Forest Service and the Shasta Nation, quotes Edward Spicer's definition of cultural perseverance and continuance: "'The persistence or stability of a people lies in the constancy of the successive interpretations with one another. If together they make up a single interrelated set of meanings through many generations then the phenomenon of the enduring people emerges'" (Winthrop 1986, 44).

The Shastas' endurance has taken many forms, including formal and informal gatherings of the people to sing, dance, and pray. One informant, describing some of these gatherings in the 1930s, stressed that the gatherings were a time for elders to give traditional prayers and for the people to talk "about the families..., where certain people live[d] at, and all these different things that pertained to the Shasta people. This is how their knowledge was passed down, from one generation to the other" (Carroway George quoted in Winthrop 1986, 60). Evidence of the endurance of the Shastan tribes' culture is their continued use of traditional healing methods and shamanic practices; their commitment to and respect for their homeland and ancestral burial sites; and their continuation of traditional forms of dress and decoration, which they adapted to the anglicized styles required by the nineteenth-century reservation officials.

Today's Shasta Nation comprises descendants of Shasta, Okwanuchu, New River Shasta, and Konomihu forebears. Of the 1,200 listed in 1986 on the tribal rolls, over 300 live on their ancestral lands. Many are involved in fighting for federal recognition and for preservation of traditional lands and lifeways. In addition to their political activity, Shastas today are active in the fields of education, medicine, farming, ranching, and business.

Susan and Jake. Courtesy of Siskiyou County Historical Society.

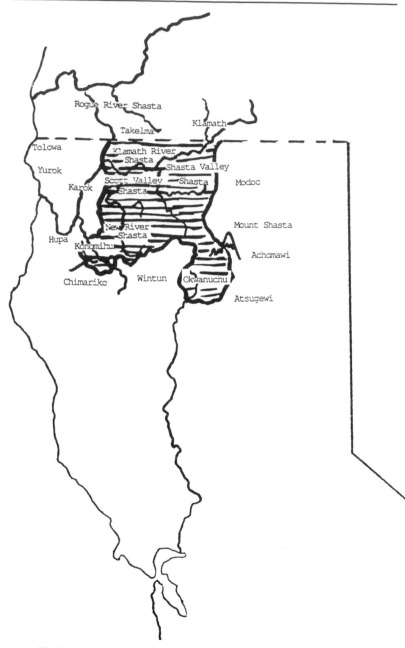

Northern California tribes.

Chapter 5

The Shastan Tribes' Neighbors

Many of the tribes whose traditional territories were adjacent to the Shasta have managed to survive the consequences of the gold rush and the white settlement of northern California, and have maintained their cultural identities. Their lands, their lifeways, and their relationships with the Shasta, however, have gone through much change. The following descriptions of the cultures and situations of these groups before white contact, as well as some of the names the tribes had for one another, are drawn from accounts of ethnographers.

Northern Neighbors: Takelma and Rogue River Athabascans

According to most accounts, the Shasta, both the California and the Oregon Rogue River bands, were often in conflict over territory with the neighboring Oregon tribes. These tribes, the Takelma and Rogue River Athabascans, lived northwest of the Klamath River Shasta and even between the Oregon and California Shasta bands. They spoke languages quite distinct from the Hokan linguistic family to which the Shastan language belongs. The Takelma called the Shasta *Wulh* or *Wulx* ("enemies").

Culturally, however, these northern tribes shared many similarities with the Shasta, with whom they traded dentalium shells for acorn flour and with whom, according to one account, they often intermarried. The Shasta, especially the Oregon Rogue River band, also put aside intertribal territorial hostilities to join forces with these northern neighbors in the fights against the whites in the mid-1800s. These battles reached their peak during the Rogue River Wars of 1855–1856, after which the tribes involved were forcibly removed to the Siletz and Grande Ronde reservations in western Oregon.

As was true for the Shasta, before white contact the family and the village were the main social units for the Takelma. Houses were partially subterranean, though unlike the similarly constructed Shasta house, entrance was made by a notched ladder through a door near the structure's roof. The sweathouse was an important part of the Takelma culture, though it was used primarily by the men. Marriages, chieftainship, and the resolution of disputes were all determined by payments and wealth.

Dress for both men and women was similar to that of the Shastan tribes. Takelma men wore buckskin breechclouts, adding leggings and shirts in cooler weather. They tattooed dentalium string measurement marks inside their forearms. Women wore the skirts and aprons of the northern California tribes, as well as the characteristic basket caps. The three tattooed chin stripes that the Shasta women wore were also common among the Takelma.

The Takelma people's diet was heavily dependent upon acorns and salmon, though like the Shasta they also ate wild roots, nuts, and berries, and hunted deer and other game. Fishermen used lines, spears, and nets, and hunters used both bows and arrows and the deer drive. The Takelma carried, stored, and prepared their food in baskets, and fashioned utensils from wood, bone, and horn.

In religion and ritual, the Takelma were again similar to the Shasta in girls' puberty ceremonies, first salmon observances, belief in charms, and shamanic practices. Takelma religious figures included "dreamers," who garnered their powers from supernatural beings other than those relied upon by the shamans. Takelma mythology includes Coyote (*Daldal*), the trickster-hero.

Eastern Neighbors: Klamath and Modoc

The Klamath and Modoc tribes are closely related to one another both in language (each belonging to the Lutuamian group) and in culture. While their traditions and lifeways show many similarities to those of the Shastan tribes, the Klamath and Modoc are more often classified within the Columbia Plateau Culture area rather than the Californian by anthropologists. The Klamath occupied the territory northeast of the Shasta, roughly above the Oregon-California border, and the Modoc held the lands in California east of the Cascades.

While the two tribes called themselves *Maklaks* ("people"), they also separately identified each other. The Klamath were called *Eukshikni Maklaks* ("Klamath Marsh People") and the Modoc were called *Moatokni Maklaks* ("Tule Lake People"). According to Kroeber ([1925] 1976), the Shasta called the Modoc *P'hanai* and the Klamath *Makaitserk*, though Holt (1946, 302) gives *Ipaxanai* (from *ipxana*, meaning "lake") as the name the Shasta used for the Modoc. The Modoc's and Klamath's name for the Shasta was *Sasti* or *Chasti*.

Interaction between the Shasta and the Oregon Klamath was minimal, but conflict between the Modoc and the Shasta was common, as the more warlike Modoc frequently made raids on the Shasta, particularly on the bands in Shasta Valley and along the Klamath River, to take women and children as slaves for themselves and for trade to northern tribes for horses. Some historians theorize, however, that these raids only became common after white incursions disrupted the traditional lifeways and stability of the Indians.

The territories of the Modoc and the Klamath peoples were primarily lands of lakes and marshes, which yielded waterfowl, fish, roots, and seeds (especially of the yellow waterlily, *wokas*, which formed their staple food). Because of the number of lakes and marshes, the Modoc and Klamath were skilled at constructing wooden canoes, as well as tule rafts. Tules were also used extensively for basketry and for clothing, which was in some ways similar to that worn by the Shasta, though often fashioned from woven tules instead of skins. The Modoc women, however, did not wear the basket caps or fringed aprons that were common among most northern California tribes, and the buckskin clothing the Modoc fashioned was more fitted than the traditional Shasta deerskin clothing. The Modoc and Klamath tribes' clothing, as well as such customs as flattening an infant's forehead and back of the skull, show influences from northern tribes along the Columbia River.

The Modoc's partially excavated winter homes differed from those of the Shastan tribes in that they were conical, with the smokehole and entrance (reached via a notched pole) at the structure's peak. Their summer homes were rectangular brush shelters of willow branch frames with grass and tule mat coverings. The Modoc's traditional sweathouse, like the Shasta's, was partially subterranean, rectangular, and brush-covered, though Plains Indians later introduced the dome-shaped, blanket-covered form, which the Modoc then passed on to the Shasta. Also unlike the traditional practice in northern California, steam rather than dry heat was used in the sweathouse. This practice, too, spread to the Shasta.

Many of the social and religious beliefs of these eastern neighbors are similar to those of the Shastan tribes. The Modoc and Klamath tribes, like most California tribes, held extended puberty rites and dances for girls. Individuals fasted and went alone on vision quests (called *spoto*), and shamans treated illnesses through a ritual that involved sucking out a foreign object. Modoc mythology features the familiar trickster-hero figure called *Kmukamch*

("Ancient Old Man"), his son *Aishish* ("Silver Fox"), and the brothers, Marten and Weasel. In funerary rites, the Klamath and Modoc tribes differed from the Shasta in that they cremated their dead, though mourners followed the same custom of painting their faces with pitch.

Southeastern Neighbors: The Achomawi

The traditional Achomawi territory lay along the Pit River and its tributaries, ranging from Montgomery Creek northward to Goose Lake. Their villages clustered along the river and streams, since the rest of the territory was mountainous and fairly barren. The Achomawi, also called the Pit River Indians, are included by early ethnographers in the Shastan group, though later studies of both language and culture show them to be a distinct though related group. Their language is in the same Hokan language family as Shastan, and their culture shows many elements similar to the culture of the Shasta.

The name "Achomawi" comes from *achuma*, meaning "river," though the tribe itself may have used that name only for the bands living in the Fall River basin. The Atsugewi to the south called the Achomawi *Pomarii*, which means "People Speaking the Same Language." The Modoc, whom the Achomawi called *Alami*, called them *Moatwas* ("Southerners"), and raided and took slaves from them. The Wintu gave the Achomawi the generic name for "foreigners" or "enemies," *Yuki*, though the Wintu also called those lowest on the Pit River *Puisu* or *Pushush*, meaning "Easterners," and apparently carried on friendly trade with them. The Achomawi called the Shasta *Sastichi*, and they referred to the neighboring Okwanuchu as *Yeti*, from the Achomawi name for Mt. Shasta, *Yet*, and some trade was carried on among these groups, too. The Shasta name for the Achomawi was *Uchahiru-tsu-his*, meaning "Far-downstream People."

The name "Pit" for both the river and the tribe comes from the Achomawi's technique of trapping deer in concealed pits, six- to nine-feet deep, which they dug along the river. Their diet also included ducks, which they snared; rabbits, which they caught in nets; salmon, trout, and suckers, which were variously netted, harpooned, and trapped. Plant foods included acorns, though these were in short supply for the eastern bands, as well as wild seeds, roots, and berries.

Their winter dwellings were partially subterranean and of bark, but the Achomawi summer homes were often in the open, perhaps beneath or behind a brush or tule mat shade. Tipis covered with tule mats have also been described by some ethnographers.

In other aspects of their culture, the Achomawi were very similar to the Shastan tribes. Clothing and ornamentation were much the same, though chin tattooing for women was not as widespread, and women occasionally wore long deerskin dresses in the Shoshonean style. Gambling was popular, with the men playing the common grass and stick games, and the women playing with mussel-shell dice. Women also played a game of shinny, and the men played a form of soccer with a ball made of deerskin stuffed with grass or hair. Brides were paid for, but the young women seem to have had some say in the choice of their spouses.

Ceremonies were few, but included girls' puberty rites and vision-seeking as part of a boy's initiation into manhood. The more powerful shamans were generally men, though both males and females practiced, and rituals included curing by sucking out pains. *Qan*, Silver Fox, was the creator figure, and *Jemul*, Coyote, was the initial bringer of all customs, as well as death and sickness.

Southern Neighbors: The Wintu and the Chimariko

Directly to the south of the Shastan tribes lived the northernmost branch of the widespread Wintun-speaking peoples. The Shasta called the Wintu *Hatukwiwa* or *Hatukeyu*, and the two tribes traded pine nuts, buckskin, dentalium shells, obsidian, and acorns. The Shasta and Wintu also occasionally fought one another, and twentieth-century Shasta informants remembered battles in the area of Callaghan, near Castle Crags, and on the Sacramento River near Antler (in Wintu territory). Several names have been recorded for the Shasta by the Wintu: *Way Yuki* ("North Enemy"), *Waikenmuk*, and *Sa-te*.

The Wintu were hill dwellers, living around the lower Pit and McCloud rivers, and the upper Sacramento and Trinity rivers in conical, bark-covered dwellings in colder months, and in brush shelters near fishing and gathering grounds in the warmer months. Acorn meal, seeds, nuts, and berries, as well as salmon, deer, and other mammals were part of the Wintu diet.

Many aspects of the Wintu culture are quite similar to the Shasta's: basic clothing, women's chin tattooing, the use of sweathouses, shamans who healed by sucking out illness-causing "pains," the girls' puberty ceremony. Wintu religious and ceremonial observances differed, however, in their detailed creation stories, which center around *Olelbis* ("He Who Is Above"), the creator figure. Another major difference lay in the Wintu's elaborate *Kuksu* cult, which involved male initiation and earth renewal rites conducted in ceremonial earth-covered lodges. Although this practice was most prevalent among the southern divisions of the Wintu, the involvement of the northern Wintu made them natural conduits for the Ghost Dance movements of the 1870s, particularly the Big Head Cult, with its emphasis on headdresses, dreamers, and the long foot-drum.

The Chimariko, one of the smallest distinct tribes in America, occupied a territory along approximately twenty miles of the Trinity River, between Hupa and Wintu lands, and directly south of the New River Shasta. The Chimariko language, like the Shastan, belongs to the Hokan language group. During the gold rush the mountainous and forested Chimariko territory was overrun with miners, who massacred most of the tribe. The remaining Chimariko took refuge with the Shasta until the miners had exhausted the gold resources, by which time few Chimariko still existed to return to their country.

Chimariko is the tribe's own name for itself, coming from *chimar* or *chimal*, meaning "person." The Hupa called them *Yinah-chin* ("Upstream People"), and, according to one source, the Shasta called them *Kwoshonipu*. One recorded Chimariko name for the Shastan people is *Hunomnichu*, though it is not clear whether this referred to the New River Shasta or the Konomihu.

The Chimariko culture shared elements common to Shastan and Hupa peoples. Social status was tied to wealth, and both disputes and marriages were settled by payments. Chimariko clothing was similar to that worn by other tribes of the area, including basket caps and fringed aprons for women, and buckskin trousers and robes for the men. Both sweathouses and dwellings were round, earth-over-madrone-bark structures. The village was governed by a headman whose position was hereditary.

Not much is known about Chimariko religious and ceremonial practices. They had both herbal doctors and sucking shamans, sweat dances, and a yearly summer dance. A girl's maturity was celebrated with a ten-day rite that was held two years after the attainment of puberty. Their mythology includes the central figure of Dog, as well as Coyote and other animal-people, and a story of a primal flood. The Chimariko people were created through the union of the one man who survived the flood and a girl who grew to life from a bone fragment that had lodged in Frog's canoe during the flood.

Western Neighbors: Hupa and Karuk

The Hupa territory touched the southwestern corner of the lands occupied by the New River Shasta and Konomihu. They were a river valley people, with their villages primarily located along the east bank of the lower Trinity River in the Hoopa Valley. The Hupa language belongs to the Athabascan group, though the tribe's culture has greater similarity to the cultures of its closest neighbors, the coastal Yurok (of the Algonquin language group) and the mountain-dwelling Karuk (of the Hokan language group).

The Shasta people did not have a great deal of contact or trade with the Hupa, since their shared boundaries encompassed the lands of the poorer Shastan tribes. Further, the Shasta regarded the Hupa with distrust, calling them "Devil People" and attributing to them the appearance of evil spirits and witches.

According to Edward Curtis, the Hupa called the Shasta *Tlomitahwe*, which is close to the name C. Hart Merriam gives as the New River Shasta's name for themselves (*Tlohomtahoi*). Kroeber, however, gives that as the name the Hupa had for the Chimariko, and states that the Hupa called the Shasta *Kiintah*. Merriam gives *Ahmutakwe* and *Etahchin* ("Easterners") as the Hupa names for the New River Shasta. The name "Hupa" comes from the Yurok name for their valley. According to Kroeber, the Hupa's name for themselves is *Natinnoh-hoi* (after Natinnoh, the Trinity River), while the Shasta called the Hupa *Chiparahihu*.

The Karuk (meaning "upstream" in the Karuk language) were the Shasta's neighbors directly to the west, in the area between the Marble Mountains and the middle stretch of the Klamath River, along which most of the Karuk villages were located. Sharing a good many cultural elements and a basic linguistic stock, the Karuk and Shasta traded heavily and apparently intermarried. The Karuk originally called themselves *Arara*, meaning "people," and referred to the Shasta individually by bands. For example, *Kakamichwi-arara* designated the Klamath River Shasta, *Tishra-w-arara* the Scott Valley Shasta, and *Mashu-arara* the New River Shasta and Konomihu. The Shasta called the Karuk *Iwapi*.

The Hupa and Karuk cultures emphasized individual wealth as a mark of social position, and while inherited position was considered, each individual's industry and thrift were also stressed. Disputes and marriages were settled by payment. Despite the Karuk emphasis on the accumulation of personal wealth, the culture also stressed the individual's responsibility to be generous and to be modest about his or her belongings.

A complex system of belief in magic, supernatural beings, and mythology characterized these two northwest coast cultures, and, as a result, the tribes had more ritual observances and ceremonies than have been recorded for the Shasta. Most of these were tied to the central belief in a prehuman race of beings that, upon the coming of the human race, removed to a mystic land across the ocean. Karuk and Hupa world renewal ceremonies involved the repetition of elaborate rituals prescribed by these beings. The ceremonies included the White Deerskin dances in the fall, at the time of the second salmon run and the acorn harvest, and Jumping dances in the spring when the salmon first started their run. Like the Shasta, the Karuk celebrated girls' puberty rites, and they observed detailed taboos in connection with such events as fishing and hunting, childbirth, and funerals. Both tribes had primarily female shamans, as well as herb doctors of either sex.

Foods, hunting and fishing practices, and clothing were all similar to those of the Shasta. Karuk and Hupa dwellings, however, were more elaborate. The living house was occupied primarily by the women and children of a family, while the men and older boys slept in the village sweathouse. The family house was a partially subterranean rectangular or square structure made of cedar planks, fronted by a stone-paved porch. The front door was low, and at ground level, with a plank ladder just inside leading down to the living area. The men's sweathouses were similar in structure to the family dwellings, though they had separate doors for entering and leaving.

Glossary

Before white contact, the people of the Shasta Nation were spread over almost all of modern-day Siskiyou county, as well as parts of Jackson and Klamath counties in Oregon. Given this geographical range and the cultural variation (albeit generally minor) among the four main tribes (Okwanuchu, New River Shasta, Konomihu, and Shasta) and even among the four main Shasta bands, it is not surprising that several different dialects developed. Ethnologists and linguists have drawn their studies of the Shastan language primarily from informants of the Shasta bands, including representatives from the Klamath Valley, the Rogue River, Scott Valley, and Shasta Valley groups, but dialectal differences are still apparent.

Three accounts of numerals illustrate some of these dialectal variations. The first column, from Catharine Holt's *Shasta Ethnology* (1946), is based on information from Sargeant Sambo, a Shasta who was born and lived most of his adult life in the Klamath River valley between Horse Creek and Hornbrook. The words in the second column are taken from Edward S. Curtis' *The North American Indian*, vol. 13 (1924). His informant for the Shastan language was Indian Jake, who was born in the Rogue River area but who was living near Yreka in 1915 when Curtis interviewed him. The third column is taken from Stephen Powers' *Tribes of California* (1877) and is from an unnamed informant from the Scott Valley band. Note that some ethnographers made use of hyphenation to clarify syllabic breaks and pronunciation; *the hyphens should not be read as pauses.*

Counting

Informant	Holt's	Curtis'	Powers'[*]
one	chaa	cha-am-mu	cha-mo
two	huk'wa	hu-ka	hu-ka
three	hachki	hats-ki	hats-ki
four	irahaia	i-ru-hai-yu	id-i-hoi-a
five	acha	e-ch-u	etch-a
ten	achahawi	e-chi-he-wi	etch-e-weh
fifty		hu-ka-his-tuq-e-chi-he-wi	
fifty	huk'wahis 'chimi achahawi		
one hundred	achahis	e-cha-his	

Other Vocabularies

The vocabulary used in the brief narrative passages in chapter two is, for consistency, taken almost exclusively from Curtis' informant. Additional vocabulary from that source follows:

Parts of the Body

arm	ha-tsar	leg	ha-ra-wai
head	cha-ro	face	an-nip-su-kuk
eye	u-wi	ear	u-wi
heart	hi-wa-sut	hair	in-nuh
breath	ke-e-su-rik		

Animals, Birds, Fish

antelope	i-yu-hi	blue jay	chas-kwai
deer	a-ro	mallard duck	kas-sa
elk	hu-ta-ka	pheasant	pis-pis
grizzly bear	ats-se	crow	a-ha-ha
mountain lion	his-si	hawk	a-ha-ku-na
coyote	kwa-tak	eagle	a-chup-ha
dog	ha-psu	quail	ta-ka-ka
fox	ku-nap-si	grouse	hu-quk

[*] Powers' list does not go beyond ten.

wolf . . . . . *tsi-wa*
jack rabbit . . *hu-wa-ha*
rattlesnake . . *hu-wa-tir*
lizard . . . . . *ta-ma-tsi*

salmon . . . . *ki-tar* or *its-mun-na*
steelhead . . . *ki-ta-rik-nuk*
trout . . . . . *ch-as*
mussel . . . . *chah-nu*

Directions, Seasons, Natural Phenomena

east . . . . . . *ka-tai-yuq*
west . . . . . *chap-hu-tu-hu*
north . . . . . *wi-ru-tu*
south . . . . . *hu-qa-tu-tu-hu*
spring . . . . *i-tu-na*
summer . . . *a-ta-hi*
autumn . . . . *wu-qu-hai*
winter/year . . *wu-qi*
dawn . . . . . *ka-ma*
evening . . . . *a-ruk*
star . . . . . . *ha-qa-sur*
earth . . . . . *ta-rak*
sky . . . . . . *qa-hu-we*
darkness . . . *i-qi-chu-hwi*
shadow . . . . *ap-hui-ha*
rock . . . . . *its-sa*
sun . . . . . . a-tsai-tsu-tsu-war

lightning . . . *i-ra-chum-mu*
thunder . . . . *ik-hi-um-me*
rain . . . . . . *i-ra-ki*
snow . . . . . *ka-u*
wind . . . . . *as-ka*
ice . . . . . . *i-yu-a*
fog . . . . . . *i-chu-ku-ru-ha*
moon . . . . . *ap-ha-tsu-tsu-war*
day . . . . . . *a-tsai*
night . . . . . *ap-ha*
lake/ocean . . *ip-ha-na*
river . . . . . *a-ti-tai-wi*
mountain . . . *wu-qe*
rainbow . . . . *chu-ku-ru-was-su*
cloud . . . . . *hi-pa-ku*
tree . . . . . . *a-ka-ha*

Wild Plant Foods and Medicines

shelled acorns (any kind) . . . . *ku-pi-ha-rik*
shelled dried acorns (any kind) . . . . *kits-su-rai*
acorn meal (unleached) . . . . *kuk-ki*
acorn meal (leached) . . . . *ka-pu*
acorn soup . . . . *si-hi-mik*
blackberries . . . . *he-ha-tu-a-tsik*
camas lily bulb . . . . *suq*
grapes . . . . *wun-tah*
hazelnuts . . . . *has-suk*
manzanita berries (black) . . . . *wa-ha*
manzanita berries (red) . . . . *has-sur*
sugar pine nuts . . . . *ats-sa-u*
plums . . . . *at-ka*
tule roots . . . . *ha-pa-ris*

wild celery root . . . . *ik-ni*
sunflower root . . . . *qa-ra-wi-hu*
wild grass seeds . . . . *hu-wa-ir-hi-hu*
tobacco . . . . *u-wa*

Objects, Qualities, Concepts

food . . . . *kits-huk*
dwelling house . . . . *um-ma*
assembly house . . . . *ok-wa-um-ma*
menstrual hut . . . . *wap-sa-hu-um-ma*
sweathouse . . . . *wuk-wu*
village ("many houses") . . . . *is-si-tu-am-ma*
tattoo . . . . *kip-ti*
basket cap . . . . *a-tsik*
deerskin skirt . . . . *chu-ri-pa*
headband . . . . *ha-ru-wa-kik*
shirt . . . . *han-ni-te-e-ma*
breechclout . . . . *ha-ta-kats-nik*
apron . . . . *hah-yi*
robe . . . . *is-se-ke*
fiber skirt . . . . *ha-i*
moccasins . . . . *ha-chah*
leggings . . . . *ha-ku-ai*
snowshoes . . . . *mi-ri*
dentalium shells . . . . *ka-qi-tik*
belt . . . . *hi-ya-mu-i*
quiver . . . . *a-u-qi-ra*
knife . . . . *ha-tsi-rai*
arrow . . . . *ak-kir*
bow . . . . *ha-u*
arrow point . . . . *ha-qai*
awl . . . . *a-hwa*
mortar . . . . *ha-tiu*
spoon . . . . *is-qai*
fish trap . . . . *a-huts-su-qa-ik*
fish weir . . . . *a-ka-hik*
storage basket . . . . *muq-sa*
baby basket . . . . *hits-si-pai-ruq*
burden basket . . . . *ha-no*

basket dish . . . . *yu-puq*
cooking basket . . . . *chi-ma-us*
tule mat . . . . *kik-hi-ya-vik*
fire drill base . . . . *hu-ro*
fire drill spindle . . . . *hu-ro-vir*
scratching stick . . . . *hi-sak*
pipe . . . . *ap-su*
deer rattle . . . . *hu-hu-pi*
dance . . . . *kus-te-hem-pik*
song . . . . *kats-nik*
dream . . . . *ki-haik*
the Great Spirit . . . . *Wa-ka*
spirit (ghost) . . . . *sum-tu*
spirit(s) (of nature) . . . . *a-xa-i-ki*
                                                  or *a-he-ki*
good . . . . *ka-ri-sa*
bad . . . . *ka-ri-qu-ch-i*
large . . . . *kim-pi*
small . . . . *a-tuq-hi-uh*
long . . . . *u-qu-ha-wi*
short . . . . *i-hi-ku*
black . . . . *ap-hu-ta-ra-hi*
red . . . . *e-eh-ti*
yellow/green . . . . *i-chum-pa-he*
white . . . . *i-ta-yu*

More Vocabulary in the Klamath River Dialect

Catharine Holt (1946) and Shirley Silver (1966), who both used Sargeant Sambo as their primary informant, include in their vocabularies complete sentences and phrases in the Klamath River band's dialect, as well as a more complete listing of terms of kinship. Here is a brief selection:

Kinship Terms

brother (man or woman speaking) . . . . *kariwa*
older brother (child speaking) . . . . *ahuhi*
younger brother, sister, or cousin (adult speaking of child) *a'chuki*
sister (man speaking) . . . . *kwaku*
older sister or girl cousin (child speaking) . . . . *achuna*
sister or girl cousin (woman speaking) . . . . *achi*
father (man or woman speaking) . . . . *ata*
(my) wife/woman . . . . (*yapu*) *tari-chi*
(my) husband/man . . . . (*yapu*) *awati'kwa*
paternal grandfather (man or woman speaking) . . . . *atsmu*
paternal grandmother (man or woman speaking) . . . . *amu*
maternal grandfather (man or woman speaking) . . . . *akwid*
maternal grandmother (man or woman speaking) . . . . *achwit*

Selected Phrases

the winter big moon . . . . *wukwitsu tchuar iknuk*
The spring moon is out now. . . . . . . *Itna'tsu tchuar gus gutsdjei.*
It is a full moon now. *Gus gwa-tin-tin*
Now winter is here. . . . . *Gus wukwi gwihiuk.*
a river bank downstream . . . . *wap-akni-ka*
mountain country . . . . *wak-we e-ki*
I sang. . . . . *Kwe-cna.*
I ate. . . . . *Kwickwa.*
We'll eat. . . . . *Cicku sa.*
We got through dancing. . . . . *Yustehempicwa.*
They are all fighting. . . . . *Kwam-ari-we-ke.*
Let's watch the gambling. . . . . *I-ya ce-kaha kehetap-ik.*
Please tell me about it. . . . . *Tahacu kim-akwaya-yak.*
You drink it up. . . . . *Kica-ci.*
He's going to get whipped. *Yam-ar.*
He went out that way. . . . . *Kwi-ackwik.*
He's running. . . . . *Kwehe-tik.*
You pick it up! . . . . *Ni-icwik-a.*
He's dressed and ready to go. . . . . *Rehiyawac-a.*
What are you saying? . . . . *Ya-a ku-ca isa tis-ay.*
He's sure dressed up! . . . . *Makay rikaha-kwaya.*

Place Names in the Shastan Language

Big Humbug Creek . . . . *Tatsu'gaho*
Black Mountain . . . . *Mahohrik*
Bogus Creek . . . . *Asura* (Ah-soo-rah) ("pale manzanita")
Cottonwood Creek . . . .*Awukha* (also *Okwayiq*)
Greenview (area around) . . . . . *Warikwi'aka* (Wa-re-kwi-ah-kah)
Hamburg (area around) . . . . *Aika*
Henley Flat . . . . *Kohapira*
Horse Creek . . . . *Itiwukhatoh*
Indian Creek (in Scott Valley) . . . .*Irui* (I-roo-ee)
Klamath Lake . . . .*Auksi*
Klamath River . . . . *Wasudigwa* (Rogue River dialect)
Little Shasta Butte . . . . .Witihassa ("crotched")
Moffett Creek . . . .*Asuri* (Ah-soo-ree)
Mount Hood . . . . *Makaiah*
Mount Shasta . . . . *Wyeka* (also spelled "Waiika")
Mugginsville (area around) . . . .*Utitapo* (Oo-tee-ta-po)
Oak Bar . . . . *Ishui* (Ish-shu-wee)
Rogue River Valley . . . . *Ikiruk*
Scott Bar . . . . *Asupak*
Scott River . . . . *Kowatsaha*
Scott Valley . . . . *Iruai* (also *It-to-wi*)
Shasta Valley . . . . *Ahotida'e*
Shasta Valley (around Montague) . . . . *Ahutirie*
Shasta Valley (area above Montague) . . . . *Upikuqah*
Sheep Rock . . . . *Kwitsa*
Shovel Creek . . . .*Asurahowa*
Table Rock . . . . *Kurutataga* (Koo-roo-tah-tah-gah)
Willow Creek . . . . *Asta*
Yreka . . . . *Uqati-amma* ("many houses")
Yreka Valley and Creek . . . . *Kusta* (Koos-tah)

Konomihu Places and Names

Black Bear Creek .... *Chupahpan'asurikaha*
(*asurikaha* means "creek")
Forks of Salmon .... *Wasuri'awa*
Indian Creek .... *Huwituk'asurikaha*
Knownothing Creek .... *Tepoi'asurikaha*
Methodist Creek .... *Kotsetsa'asurikaha*
North Fork of Salmon River .... *Okohoro*
Plummer Creek .... *Hupoho'asurikaha*
Salmon River .... *Kohapa*
South Fork of Salmon River .... *Wasurekwiaka*

Selected Bibliography and Suggested Readings

Anthony, E. M. "Reminiscences in Siskiyou County." 1969. Bancroft Library, University of California, Berkeley. Manuscript.

Bancroft, Hubert Howe. *The Native Races*, vol. 1, *Wild Tribes*. Chapter IV, "Californians"; and vol. 3, "Myths and Languages." San Francisco: A. L. Bancroft, 1883.

Brandon, William. *The American Heritage Book of Indians*. New York: American Heritage, 1961.

Bright, William and David L. Olmsted. *A Shasta Vocabulary*. Kroeber Anthropology Society Papers, vol. 20:1-55. Berkeley: University of California Press, n.d.

Burns, L. M. "Digger Indian Legends." *Land of Sunshine*, vol. 14 (1901): 130-34, 223-26, 310-14, 397-402.

Clark, Ella C. *Indian Legends of the Pacific Northwest*. Berkeley: University of California Press, 1953.

Coffin, Tristram P., editor. *Indian Tales of North America*. Philadelphia: American Folklore Society, 1961.

Curtis, Edward S. *The North American Indian*, vol. 13. Cambridge: The University Press, 1924.

Curtin, J. "Achomawi Myths." *Journal of American Folklore*, vol. 22 (1909).

Dillon, Richard. *Siskiyou Trail: The Hudson's Bay Company Route to California*. New York: McGraw-Hill, 1975.

Dixon, Roland B. "The Mythology of the Shasta-Achomawi." *American Anthropologist*, vol. 7 (1905): 607-12.

_____. "Notes on the Achomawi and Atsugewi of Northern California." *American Anthropologist*, vol. 10 (1908): 208-20.

_____. "Achomawi and Atsugewi Tales." *Journal of American Folklore*, vol. 21 (1908).

_____. "Shasta Myths." *Journal of American Folklore*, vol. 23 (1910).

_____. "The Shasta." Huntington Expedition Report. *Bulletin of the American Museum of Natural History*, vol. 17, part 5 (1907).

DuBois, Cora. *The 1870 Ghost Dance*. University of California Anthropological Records, vol. 3. Berkeley: University of California Press, 1946.

Farrand, Livingston. "Shasta and Athapascan Myths from Oregon." Edited by Leo Frachtenberg. *Journal of American Folklore*, vol. 28 (1915): 207-43.

Forbes, Jack D. *Native Americans of California and Nevada*. Happy Camp, California: Naturegraph Publishers, 1969.

Gatschet, Albert S. "Sasti-English and English-Sasti Dictionary," 1877. Manuscript no. 706 in the National Anthropological Archives, Smithsonian Institution, Washington D.C.

Gibbs, George. *George Gibb's Journal of Redick McKee's Expedition Through Northwestern California in 1851*. Edited and annotated by Robert F. Heizer. University of California Archaeological Research Facility. Berkeley: University of California Press, 1972.

Gridley, Marion. *Indian Legends of American Scenes*. Chicago: M. A. Donohue, 1939.

Gifford, Edward W. and Gwendoline Harris Block. *California Indian Nights Entertainment*. Glendale, California: Arthur H. Clark, 1930.

Heizer, Robert F. *The Eighteen Unratified Treaties of 1851-1852 between the California Indians and the United States Government*. University of California Archaeological Research Facility. Berkeley: University of California Press, 1972.

_____. *Languages, Territories, and Names of California Indian Tribes*. Berkeley: University of California Press, 1966.

Heizer, Robert F. and Thomas R. Hester. *Shasta Villages and Territory*. University of California Archaeological Research Facility Contributions, vol. 9, no. 6. Berkeley: University of California Press, 1970.

_____. "Treaties" in *Handbook of North American Indians*, vol. 8, *California*. Washington: Smithsonian Institution, 1978.

Heizer, Robert F. and M. A. Whipple, editors. *The California Indians: A Source Book*, 2nd ed. Berkeley: University of California Press, 1971.

Holsinger, Rosemary. *Shasta Indian Tales*. Happy Camp, California: Naturegraph Publishers, 1982.

Holt, (Permelia) Catharine. *Shasta Ethnology*. University of California Anthropological Records, vol. 3, no. 4. Berkeley: University of California Press, 1946.

_____. "The Relations of Shasta Folklore," 1942. Doe Library, University of California, Berkeley. Ph.D. dissertation.

_____. "Shasta Myths," 1937. Bancroft Library, University of California, Berkeley. Manuscript.

Howe, Carroll. *Ancient Tribes of the Klamath Country*. Portland, Oregon: Binford & Mort, 1968.

Jones, J. Roy. *Saddle Bags in Siskiyou*. Happy Camp: Naturegraph Publishers, 1980 [reprint of 1953 edition].

Judson, Katharine B. *Myths and Legends of California and the Old Southwest*. Chicago: A. C. Clurg, 1912.

Knudtson, Peter. *The Wintun Indians of California and Their Neighbors*. Happy Camp: Naturegraph Publishers, 1977.

Kroeber, A. E. *Handbook of the Indians of California*. New York: Dover Publications, 1976 [reprint of 1925 edition].

_____. *Yurok Myths*. Berkeley: University of California Press, 1976.

Kroeber, Theodora. *The Inland Whale*. Berkeley: University of California Press, 1959.

Laland, Jeffrey. *First Over the Siskiyous: A Commentary on Peter Skene Ogden's 1826-1827 Route of Travel through Northern California and Southwestern Oregon*. Portland, Oregon: Oregon Historical Society Press, 1987.

Martin, Pat. "The Shasta." *Siskiyou Pioneer and Yearbook*, vol. 4, no. 4. Yreka, California: Siskiyou County Historical Society, 1971.

Merriam, C. Hart. Cataloged collection of unpublished field notes, manuscripts, and photographs. Bancroft Library, University of California, Berkeley.

_____. *Ethnographic Notes on California Indian Tribes*. Edited by Robert F. Heizer. University of California Archaeological Survey Reports, no. 68. Berkeley: University of California Press, 1966-1967.

_____. "Little Known Tribes of the Salmon, New and Trinity Rivers in Northern California." *Journal of the Washington Academy of Sciences*, vol. 20, no. 8 (1930): 148-49.

_____. "The New River Indians Tlo-hom-tah-hoi." *American Anthropologist*, vol. 32 (1930): 280-93.

_____. "The Source of the Name Shasta." *Journal of the Washington Academy of Sciences*, vol. 16, no. 19: 522-25.

_____. *Studies of California Indians*. Berkeley: University of California Press, 1955.

Merriam, C. Hart and Z. M. Talbot. *Boundary Descriptions of California Indian Stocks and Tribes*. University of California Archaeological Research Facility. Berkeley: University of California Press, 1974.

Miller, Joaquin. *Life Amongst the Modocs: Unwritten History*. London: Richard Bentley and Son, 1873.

Nelson, Velma. "Legends on the Origin of Mt. Shasta" in *California Folklore*, Chico Collection, vol. 13. (Unpublished manuscript collection in Meriam Library, California State University, Chico, 1947-1960.)

Powers, Stephen. *Tribes of California*. Berkeley: University of California Press, 1976 [reprint of 1877 edition].

_____. "California Indians, No. XI: Various Tribes [Achomawi, Yani, Sierra Maidu]." *Overland Monthly*, vol. 12 (1874): 412-24.

_____. "The Shasta and Their Neighbors," 1873. Bancroft Library, University of California, Berkeley. Manuscript.

Schaaf, Gregory. Interview. California State University, Chico. September 1989.

Schoolcraft, Henry Rowe. *Historical and Statistical Information Respecting the History, Condition, and Prospects of the Indian Tribes of the United States*. Vol. 3, p. 110; vol. 5, pp. 214-17 (George Gibb's travel diary from Shastan areas). Philadelphia: Lippincott, Grambo, 1851–1857 [reprint: New York: Paladin Press, 1969].

Silver, Shirley. "The Shastan Language," 1966. University of California, Berkeley. Ph.D. dissertation.

_____. "Shasta Peoples" in *Handbook of North American Indians*, vol. 8, *California*. Edited by Robert F. Heizer. Washington: Smithsonian Institution, 1978.

_____. "Shasta and Konomihu" in *Trends in Linguistics*. New York: Mouton Publishers, n.d.

Taylor, Alexander. "Indianology of California." *California Farmer and Journal of Useful Sciences*, vols. 13-20 (1860–1863).

Thornton, Russell. *We Shall Live Again: The 1870 and 1890 Ghost Dance Movements as Demographic Revitalization*. New York: Cambridge University Press, 1986.

Voegelin, Erminie. *Culture Element Distributions XX: Northeastern California*. University of California Anthropological Records, vol. 7, no. 2. Berkeley: University of California Press, 1942.

Walsh, Frank K. *Indian Battles of the Lower Rogue*. Grants Pass, Oregon: Te-cum-tom Enterprises, 1970.

Webster, Tom and Bess Webster. Unpublished interviews. Fort Jones, California, 1986–1989.

Wicks, Clara. Taped conversations in the private possession of Bess and Tom Webster, 1970s.

Wilkes, Charles. *Narrative of the U. S. Exploring Expedition: During the Years of 1838, 1839, 1840, 1841, 1842*. Philadelphia: Lea and Blanchard, 1845.

Winthrop, Robert H. *Survival and Adaptation Among the Shasta Indians*. Edited and revised by the Shasta Nation Review Committee. Prepared for the United States Forest Service, Klamath National Forest, Yreka, California. Ashland, Oregon: Winthrop Associates, 1986.